The Education of Linguistic and Cultural Minorities in the OECD Countries

Multilingual Matters

Please contact us for the latest information on recent and forthcoming books in the series.

Derrick Sharp, General Editor, Multilingual Matters,
Bank House, 8a Hill Road, Clevedon, Avon BS21 7HH, England.

MULTILINGUAL MATTERS 13

The Education of Linguistic and Cultural Minorities in the OECD Countries

Stacy Churchill

**MULTILINGUAL
MATTERS LTD**

British Library Cataloguing in Publication Data

Churchill, Stacy
    The education of linguistic and cultural
    minorities in the OECD countries.—(Multilingual
    matters; 13)
    1. Linguistic minorities—Education
    I. Title   II. Series
    371.97   LC3715

    ISBN 0–905028–34–1
    ISBN 0–905028–33–3 Pbk

Multilingual Matters Ltd.
Bank House, 8a Hill Road,
Clevedon, Avon BS21 7HH,
England.

Typeset by Photo·Graphics, Honiton, Devon
Printed and bound in Great Britain by
Short Run Press Ltd, Exeter EX2 7LW

This book is dedicated to

Prof. Torsten Husén

of Sweden, in respectful recognition of his leadership in developing comparative international studies of education and in gratitude for encouragement to the author's efforts in this field.

Acknowledgements

Background research for some parts of this book was carried out during the period January–June 1978. At that time I was on a study leave granted by the Ontario Institute for Studies in Education and, as Senior Fellow at the Centre for Educational Research and Innovation, Paris, helped to manage some parts of the project "Finance, Organisation and Governance of Education for Special Populations". Appreciation is due to both institutions for affording me this opportunity. Especial gratitude is due to Mr Beresford Hayward, of the OECD Secretariat, who after many months had passed and the project came to an end, encouraged me to take up the task of synthesizing its results related to the education of linguistic and cultural minorities. In addition he provided valuable substantive advice in shaping some of its conclusions.

Stacy Churchill

Contents

1 Introduction

This book examines the process of educational policy making in the OECD countries during the last two decades with respect to the education of linguistic and cultural minorities. The main purpose is to review the different types of policy instrument available and the consequences of the choice of different instruments.

Chapter 2 places the study in the context of earlier OECD projects, particularly the project on primary school finance. The main data sources of the current project – some 30 consultants' papers in three series: I. Country Surveys. II. Issues. III. Selected Populations – are reviewed: they demonstrate an almost universal concern of OECD countries for the educational problems of linguistic and cultural minorities. The conceptual framework of the project of Finance, Organisation and Governance of Education for Special Populations is reviewed, deficiencies are noted in the formulation, and a refinement of terminology is set out as a basis for the remainder of the analysis in this book.

Chapter 3 analyses the definition of policy objectives in different countries. The main element commanding the definition of objectives is found to be the force of majority public opinion in each country. The main background factors – minority group characteristics and the national setting – are considered along with a factor not studied in the project, the autonomous role of educators within the educational systems. The public opinion of the minorities, particularly their pressures for changes, is seen as a prime motor of policy evolution. Minority opinions are grouped into a simple typology showing their stages of development. The main factor, the weight of majority public opinion in the different countries, reposes upon a set of relatively explicit definitions of what is the nature of the educational problem faced by linguistic and cultural minorities: six stages in the development of problem definition are identified in the countries studied. Each stage of problem definition corresponds to a set of expectations about the use of the minority language and culture and to a set of typical educational practices and policy actions.

Chapter 4 is a concentrated analysis of the entire range of policy instruments available to educational decision makers and national authorities in shaping educational responses to minority group problems. The topic "legal status and framework" outlines the main options for decisions on how policy is made, who participates in the process, and who is a legitimate "client" of education; it also identifies the main factors that determine the choices of policy instrument "level" (law, regulation, circular, etc.). Organizational arrangements for education are discussed in relation to instructional provisions, administrative framework, and support and ancillary services. Under each of these headings, it is seen that (a) a clear preference "hierarchy" can be established, from least favourable to most favourable for the development of minorities as groups, (b) that these levels are linked to the stages of problem definition identified in majority public opinion (Chapter 3) and (c) that the choices made have important implications for the education received by the minorities. Financial instruments are not discussed separately but in conjunction with what are called "regulatory stances": policy makers appear to deal with finance as part of a larger policy "package" in which financial measures are co-ordinated with other policy action. A selection of 14 types of financial arrangement provides a basis for·classifying national stances with respect to degrees of central control; in turn, these stances are shown to have direct effect on the degree of educational provision made for minorities.

Chapter 5 deals with the issue of how minorities participate in, or are excluded from participation in, the governance process. A variety of levels of participation are identified, with the more meaningful ones being reserved for the older, established minorities. In addition, different governance approaches (centralized/decentralized) are discussed in the light of their implications for the provision of services to minorities.

Chapter 6 attempts to look at the logic that underlies the policies adopted in different countries, both explicit and implicit. Assumptions about the costs of provisions are examined, and it is noted that the conception most satisfactory in economic theory — opportunity costs — is usually overlooked in policy making. Costs of programmes for minorities are dealt with in accounting terms, without noting that the failure to spend money on a programme shifts the real costs to the minorities affected (lost education, income, etc.). The objectives of public policies in the OECD countries are linked to expected outcomes for the minorities and derive directly from the problem definitions identified in Chapter 3. The specific educational treatments given minorities are similarly reviewed and shown to be consistently derived from the problem definitions. These are, in turn, linked with specific conceptions of the nature and role of minority cultures. Rationales for differential allocation of resources to achieve specific policy objectives with respect to minority education are reviewed. The general principles of equity identified in the policies are well-known and have been used for other populations. The reasons why governments have extended the equity principles to linguistic and cultural minorities furnish an interesting parallel with the development of special education for the handicapped. The same historical stages are found to exist, but as minorities become recognized in certain countries and valued as members of society, additional rationales are added.

Chapter 7 attempts to draw broad conclusions about the policy making process. The earlier chapters have revealed a great consistency: minority group aspirations, majority group opinion and problem definitions, policy objectives, policy options, policy rationales — all the elements analysed — fit into a clear, consistent pattern. This regularity across the different countries suggests great underlying similarities of social processes related to institutionalized public education. The often abysmal results obtained by educational policies are traced in large measure to the limits placed by public opinion and by accepted problem definitions on the range of policy options that can be considered and adopted by authorities. The chapter concludes with suggested areas of priority for future information and research, noting the particular gravity of educational problems that afflict not only the "new" minorities but also, most acutely, the indigenous peoples.

2 A study of educational policy making and its impact on minority education

A new policy focus

Linguistic and cultural minorities have recently emerged as a central concern for educational policy in almost all the OECD countries,[1] with the sole exception of Japan. This has been documented for the first time in a cross-national study carried out under the sponsorship of the Centre for Educational Research and Innovation (CERI), an affiliate organism of the OECD. This chapter examines the main dimensions of the project entitled "Finance, Organisation and Governance of Education for Special Populations". The book as a whole is an analytical summary of its main findings on minority education. The impetus for writing it came from an examination of the initial results of the research. It had been expected that the central focus would be on groups that are traditionally dealt with as part of so-called "special education" — the handicapped, the disadvantaged, the retarded, and the gifted. A special group of studies on minorities was part of the design; the purpose was to do an initial exploration of the issues of language and culture in education. As it turned out, the general studies of national policies also took up the same theme. In the end, a separate synthesis report proved to be the only manageable way to cope with the vast array of information made available, most of it collected for the first time.

The approach taken here is radically different from that found in most studies of linguistic and cultural minorities. It is usual to select one or more minorities for study, to decide who fits the definition of the group(s), and then to examine how their problems and how they relate to the context —

4

social, political or other. Most such examinations produce, either directly or indirectly, suggestions for societal change or proposals to modify public policy to better meet minority needs. Here, however, the problem is turned around, so to speak. The *initial* focus is on public policy as it already exists and, specifically, on the process by which educational policies are defined, articulated and carried out. Thus, instead of giving our definition of which minorities were to be examined, we attempted to find out how national policy makers define them and how these definitions differ. Given the differences between countries — for example between Switzerland and Australia, to mention two jurisdictions whose policies are examined here — it is hardly surprising that definitions used for educational policy are different. What IS surprising was our discovery that, despite the surface variety of political arrangements, educational structures, and national historical traditions, policy makers and educators in the various countries shared many common concerns, even the same "technical" and administrative problems. Such commonalities often transcended structural contrasts, such as between centralized and decentralized (or federative) systems of educational administration and governance: the federated *Länder* in West Germany face decisions about the schooling of children of foreign workers that are very similar to those of the (centralized) Ministry of Education in France.

The *ultimate* focus of the study is, obviously, on the minorities themselves, on their needs and on how schools meet them, or fail to do so. Despite the strong temptation to editorialize, it has been necessary to respect the initial aim of the project, which was to provide a vantage point for understanding decision processes, not to deliver a weighty evaluation of the policies of each country, levelling criticisms here and bestowing merit points there. Such a procedure was hardly compatible with a project in which the co-operation of national authorities was a vital component. Nor was it particularly necessary: the growing awareness of minority problems in all the countries studied, has developed a relatively vast literature of this sort, obviously far more grounded in realities than one could hope to find in a single international project.

One of the consequences of the approach taken is that, even after completion of the project, it was impossible to say — even roughly — how many people belong to linguistic and cultural minorities across the OECD countries or even, for that matter, to provide a preliminary list of them. A moment's reflection is enough to understand why this must be so. As our work revealed, the groups deemed important as minorities for policy-making purposes in a country, state, or province may shift radically from time to time. Often the definition of who is, or is not, to be considered the member of a given minority is an issue of policy making, if not outright political debate (not to mention the views of the individuals concerned). Take one example from recent history: two or three generations ago, discrimination against Jews was commonplace in the educational systems of most countries where they resided; where the practice was not actively encouraged by law, enlightened educational policy makers (by our current standards) sometimes defined Jews as a special group whose needs required that policies be pursued in order to overcome the disadvantage they suffered. Despite the fact that *de facto* anti-Semitism is a vigorous and active force in many places today, there are few indications that policy makers in OECD countries feel it necessary any more to establish policies to ensure access to educational facilities for them. In fact religious differences are rarely viewed as a basis for special educational measures (except where systems of religious-based schools are already a traditional part of the national educational system). This does not mean that problems do not exist nor that further measures might not be appropriate in many specific situations, simply that in terms of most current policy, the needs of members of groups defined by religious affiliation have ceased to be a point of focus. Minorities defined in myriad ways continue to exist, even though they may slip from the forefront of current issues of policy.

With great differences of emphasis between countries, we can say that the policies reviewed here apply to three main types of minority groups.

a. *Indigenous peoples*: groups long-established in their native countries whose life style follows a traditional mode considered archaic by contemporary industrial societies. Definitions in a time of cultural change are tenuous, but it is generally agreed that this category includes Samit (Lapps), Australian aboriginal peoples, Maoris and Pacific Islanders, Native American Indians, and other "similar" groups, along with their descendants (including sometimes those of mixed ancestry).

b. *"Established" minorities*: groups long-established in their native countries whose life style has generally tended to evolve along the same lines as that of the remainder of their national society, though sometimes falling behind in the rate of evolution. Typical examples would be the Catalans in Spain, the Acadian French in the U.S., the Bretons in France, or Canadian Francophones.

c. *"New" minorities*: groups perceived to have migrated recently to their current place of residence. These persons might be immigrants in the legal sense that their move is intended to lead to a change of nationality. In Western Europe this group includes resident foreign workers who have changed countries, ostensibly on a temporary basis, even though most appear to have acquired *de facto* the status of permanent residents. Other "new" minorities are created by phenomena of internal migration within a country, a colonial state, or the limits of a former colonial entity, such as the British Commonwealth. Creation of such minorities has been fostered in some cases by the creation of interstate communities whose citizens have the right of free establishment and movement within the community, e.g. the Nordic states or the European Economic Community.

These categories are hardly precise, for the social phenomena themselves are extremely fluid in the current period of history. The gypsies of Western Europe fit almost no definition, or all of them. How, for example, does one categorize the black population of the United States? Certainly they constitute, as a group, a distinctive cultural and linguistic community, but most policies deal with them in terms of their racial characteristics; conversely, while U.S. policy recognizes persons of Hispanic speech and background in terms of their culture, it is common practice also to distinguish persons of Hispanic American ancestry from persons of other "races", e.g. from Blacks or "Caucasians". Or, in a multicultural state such as Switzerland, how does one categorize the four main recognized linguistic groupings? Do dialectical differences "count" and, if so, how big must the difference be to have implications for education? A recent report by a committee of the Parliamentary Assembly of the Council of Europe (a mainly consultative assembly) listed some 51 cases of linguistic and cultural minorities among the member states; this did not include persons such as resident foreign workers, and some of the groups were minorities within two or more countries, such as the Basques. The recommendations of the committee, adopted by the Parliamentary Assembly on 7 October 1981, requested that the Council's Committee of Ministers give consideration, among other measures, to "the gradual adoption of children's mother tongues for their education (use of dialects as the spoken language in pre-school education, and use of standardised mother-tongue language forms in primary education, the prevailing language of the country being then progressively introduced alongside the mother tongue" (Council of Europe, 1981). The recommendation amounts to little more than a polite request for such matters to be discussed, but a simple examination of the potential implications of implementing it with respect to even a few of the minorities mentioned, illustrates how complex is the interplay between human sociological realities and educational policy development for minority education. Where and how does one draw the line?

However uncertain or confusing the definitional problems may be both in theory and practice, policy making about the education of minorities must cope with an overriding fact: *almost every jurisdiction in the industrialized world is failing adequately to meet the educational needs of a significant number of members of linguistic and cultural minorities, even when measured against the limited criterion of education to the minimum necessary to have equitable chances to obtain employment. Measured against the criterion of ensuring linguistic and/or cultural survival in the long term, the shortfall is much more serious, reaching dramatic proportions most particularly in its impact on indigenous peoples.*

The problems in education are usually a partial reflection of serious social problems outside the schools, but neither public opinion nor policy makers are apparently as willing as in the past to accept this as a rationale for not adapting education better to serve the needs of underprivileged groups. It may well be that, upon completing *gymnasium* and a degree in engineering, the son of a Turkish worker resident in Bavaria might sometimes encounter difficulties in being fully accepted as the equal of an engineer of German descent, but there are few prepared to argue that the same second-generation foreign resident would be better off to receive a poor education as preparation to enter adult life. The same logic is being applied in most countries to push the search for better answers *within* the educational system.

The European policy awakening

Most of the non-European members of the OECD (Australia, Canada, New Zealand, the U.S. but not Japan) have a rather long record of dealing both with indigenous peoples and "new" minorities in the policy making process. A large part of their policy evolution of the past two decades has involved self-criticism of the results obtained and a search for new ways of addressing old problems. This is only true to a certain extent with the European states. Along with the realization that many old, established minorities are facing extinction from the inroads of modern life and its accompanying social pressures, the essentially new element in the political situation has been the growing size of the "new" minorities and the acuteness of the social and educational costs being borne by their children — the resident foreign workers in most of continental Europe and immigrants from the "new" Commonwealth in the U.K. Improvised national responses have given way gradually to a situation where educational and other social measures are being discussed in a broader cross-national framework, while more comprehensive steps are taken in each country's school system. Despite very serious efforts at exchanges within the framework of interstate organizations (Nordic Council, Council of Europe, European Economic Community, OECD), it is fair to say that even a full description of the demographic realities involved is only now beginning to emerge, and no detailed and coherent picture of educational policy and practice exists. This current volume is a first step in this direction, dealing primarily with the policy processes and frameworks but without a quantitative or qualitative assessment of results.

The most comprehensive recent treatment of the demographic factors underlying the European policy awakening is to be found in the report of an OECD working party, published under the title *Migrants' Children and Employment: The European Experience* (OECD, 1983). The study is based on a questionnaire to which eleven countries replied; using this and other information sources, the group drew a statistical picture of the "second generation" of European migrants for eight of the traditional "host" countries (Austria, Belgium, France, Germany, the Netherlands, Luxembourg, Sweden, Switzerland), and presented as well the view of the major emigration countries (Italy, Portugal, Spain, Turkey, and Yugoslavia). The U.K. is the main host country missing, but most of its migratory flows come from outside Europe; among the emigration countries, the European focus eliminated, of course, such major sources as Morocco and Algeria. Limiting itself only to young persons (25 years and under) who were foreigners in the country of residence (i.e. excluding those of foreign descent who had acquired citizenship and thus underestimating significantly the numbers involved), the report presents a picture with few bright spots. Of the 4.5 million young European residents identified, between half and three-quarters were born in the countries where their parents worked; 75 to 90% of second-generation migrants have received all their education in the country where their parents work. An additional 2 million children remained behind in the main originating countries. The young migrants are everywhere in a disadvantaged position. They are oriented in the schools towards shorter and/or less prestigious educational streams leading most directly into working life and, in particular, towards those that prepare for jobs where foreign manpower is already high. About 90% of young foreign-origin men and 60–75% of young foreign-origin women are employed as manual labourers. Despite official efforts to the contrary, many fail to enrol in school at all, e.g. an estimated 36,500 (approx.) Turkish children aged 6–15 living in Germany received no education at all in 1979–80 (OECD, 1983). An estimate for all countries of the European Economic Community set at 300,000 the figure for children who, in 1975, did not attend school or had "incomplete attendance" (cited CERI, 1983). The prospects for return of the young persons to their countries of origin are only sketched, but all indications are that few special efforts are being made to help those who return to integrate into education or work life, even though many are severely disadvantaged from inadequate knowledge of the language of their parents' home country and of its society. The conclusions of the report point to a "growing gap" between the numbers of young foreigners and their social and occupational status which "appears likely to generate serious tensions unless appropriate steps are taken". Since it is "unlikely that many young migrants will want to return to their parents' country of origin", the report urges upon the different countries a review of their policies aimed at protecting "national" manpower, such as the expulsions of unemployed youths practiced by some jurisdictions (OECD, 1983: 7–8).

The title given to the study refers to "migrants", continuing a fiction that still dominates many European political debates. Meanwhile most countries have begun at least a limited revision of their outlook but are held back by current problems of unemployment and the resistance of many sectors of public opinion to accept the legitimation of foreign workers' rights to permanency or that of the second generation to have equal access to national job opportunities. According to a recent analysis of policies and regulations, the main immigration countries (U.K. excluded from consideration) can be divided into two main groups. The first, composed of Austria, Belgium, Germany and Switzerland, continue to adhere to the principle of mobility, i.e. the expectation that foreign workers are likely to return to their homelands; this principle takes about an equal place in their policies with measures to improve the integration of foreign workers into their society. France and the Netherlands have meanwhile oriented themselves towards a line of policy pioneered by Sweden, creating a second group. Despite some hesitations, they have given the principle of integration greater prominence, as policies reflect increasing acceptance of the permanency of foreign workers. As a corollary, they are also making efforts to prepare public opinion in the host societies for a greater degree of cultural diversification.[2] The distinctions between the two groupings of countries are tenuous because, as the study notes, the laws and regulations on which the categorization is based, "in many cases have not been applied and, conversely, practices are applied for which there is no legislation". The study reflects a widespread European malaise with respect to the problem of second generation "migrants" and raises a line of questioning which, if pursued actively, may well bring related policy discussion into the mainstream of politics in all the countries: there are preliminary indications that the educational disadvantage of the children of foreign workers (as well as their difficulties in obtaining access to occupational outlets permitting upward social mobility) may sometimes prove indistinguishable from those of persons in the host society whose socio-economic background is the same. If this were the case, then the guidelines adopted for the education of children of foreign origin "would have to be seriously reviewed and the pedagogical model used up to now for the education of these pupils would have to be redesigned" (CERI, 1983: 9, 34). The net result of these orientations in policy discussion is to bring the immediate concerns and perceptions of European policy makers much closer to those of the English-speaking OECD members and Canada, where integration of new arrivals on a long-term basis has been a central focus of policy for much longer.

Serious long-term policy problems remain unresolved, and it is not possible to foresee the outcome. Thus the recognition of the "foreign-ness" of the children of so-called guest workers has permitted all the major host countries to subscribe formally to a Council of Europe recommendation that they should have access to instruction in their mother tongue; depending upon the country and language groups involved, this is being more or less widely applied. This breach in the dominance of official national languages as media of instruction breaks with all tradition and opens the way for discussions of multiculturalism in a broader sense. However, if public opinion becomes broadly convinced of the permanency of the persons concerned, there is a strong possibility, indeed a near certainty, that voices will be raised to do away with access to mother tongue instruction in favour of rigid enforcement of the use of the official national languages. The present phase of mother tongue instructional policies appears very much like a set of patches applied to a few points on an otherwise uniform fabric of unilingual systems of instruction. (Bilingual and multilingual countries practice unilingualism usually within each official component of the educational system.) And, in all the debate, the U.K. has maintained its isolation: as indicated in the national case study used for the current project, official agreement to apply the Council of Europe recommendation regarding mother tongue education has virtually not been followed by measures to implement it. On the other hand, this is accompanied by numerous local initiatives that may be grouped under the heading "multiculturalism", with considerable amounts of support from majority opinion in the British population. In all the countries, the persistent problem of unemployment and economic uncertainty remains a major factor menacing progress achieved in rendering opinion favourable to these new minorities.

Structure of the project

The project "Finance, Organisation and Governance of Education for Special Populations" was structured as a series of case studies and opinion papers, some contributed by national education authorities, others commissioned from individual authors directly by the OECD Secretariat. For purposes of communication within the project, these were divided into three series (see list of references at the end of this book for a complete breakdown). The first, so-called "mapping studies", are framed around a series of major topics to which national education authorities were asked to respond. Essentially they provide a general listing, with appropriate commentaries, of the entire range of programmes established in each country to assist the education of special populations: an over-all "map" of policies. Out of these, the authors then selected a few populations, for which educational arrangements, including finance and administration, were described in greater detail. Series II is made up of commissioned opinion papers by noted experts on topics considered to be of permanent interest to policy making. For example how does autonomy of local or regional educational authorities affect provision of education? Does identifying an individual as in need of special education result in "labelling" which creates negative educational effects that reinforce already existing disadvantage? Such topics cut across the broad range of educational provisions described in the Series I papers. Series II papers became known as "issues papers". Finally, Series III is devoted to a detailed exploration of one emerging policy area, the education of linguistic and cultural minorities. It consists of a group of national case studies devoted to "new" and "established" minorities, together with a series of opinion papers on education of indigenous peoples. The latter component was structured as a broad statement of related issues ("Analytical framework") followed by commentaries on it drawn from persons expert in the field.

This project structure arose after a careful review of a previous policy analysis study carried out by CERI, issued in a series of publications under the title *Educational Financing and Policy Goals for Primary Schools* (Noah & Sherman, 1979, for summary). The results demonstrated the feasibility of comparative studies of educational policy based on very detailed descriptions of national situations using a common framework for data collection. Since it had concentrated on one sector of educational policy, the next step was felt to be a consideration of the broader range of concerns reflected by the triad of finance, organization and governance. The new study was intended to narrow and intensify the focus of research around the issue of special populations, which the finance study showed to be a particular concern of policy makers. Addressing finance, organization and governance for the whole of primary or secondary education was manifestly too much to manage as a single project.

Special populations are put under a sort of analytical microscope, with each series of papers representing a different level of "magnification". Series I papers go beyond the financial focus of the first project to permit examination of the interplay between financial instruments and other means of intervention to achieve policy goals — administrative, regulatory, and other measures — but still always within the context of the educational system. The Series II papers were intended to cut across policies to deepen understanding of key dilemmas and methodological problems of policy making in education. Series III was intended to break out of the boundaries of the educational system in order to place its problems in a much broader context showing the interaction between the realm of educational policy and other social forces, such as national traditions of literacy, the educational goals of affected population groups, and the general development of social policy. A striking demonstration of the newness of the minorities topic in the general framework of policy studies of this sort (despite the old nature of the problem) is that Series II papers generally do *not* come to grips with matters outside the usual bounds of special education as traditionally conceived. (The remarks on costing techniques by Rossmiller and on the nature of cost as a concept of economics, by Peston, can be applied to minorities without modification.)

The results of applying this design were more focused, in one sense, than might have been anticipated. Out of 15 mapping studies in Series I, 14 countries reported on policies developed for linguistic and cultural minorities (Table 1). A total of eleven chose linguistic cultural minorities within the country for detailed examination, an additional two — Portugal and Turkey — discussed programmes for their nationals abroad (where they constitute, of course, linguistic and cultural minorities), and only two — Ireland and Norway — did not deal in detail with programmes for such groups. (Within its regular schools, Ireland offers to the majority, options for study in Gaelic and English.) To complete the picture, one may note that, of the six remaining OECD countries not included in the studies, four have major institutional arrangements to accommodate linguistic diversity in their native populations (Belgium, Finland, Spain and Yugoslavia) and one (Austria) has limited bilingualism in certain areas combined with programmes for resident foreign workers. Even a country as homogeneous as Japan is demonstrating concern for matters of language, particularly with respect to resident workers of Korean origin. Thus, the discussion of the papers in Series III can be related to a much larger policy background

TABLE 1   *Linguistic and cultural minorities treated in the country surveys of current practice (Series I)*

	General Treatment	Detailed Treatment
Australia	Non-English-speaking Aborigines	Aborigines
Canada (Ontario)	Francophones Multi-cultural (immigrant or descendants) Native Peoples	Francophones Multi-cultural
Denmark	Non-Danish-Speaking (including Faroe Islanders and residents from Greenland)	Non-Danish-speaking
England and Wales	Immigrants and descendants (Urban programme) Welsh	Immigrants and descendants (Urban programme)
France	Non-French-speaking immigrants	Non-French-speaking immigrants
Germany	"Resettlers" of German Origin	
Ireland	– – –	
The Netherlands	Cultural minorities (various)	Moluccans
New Zealand	Maori and Pacific Island Peoples	Maori and Pacific Island Peoples

— the almost universal concern within OECD countries today for language and cultural problems as they affect specific minorities.

The Series III studies are structured into two major components. The first (A.) consists of national case studies in four countries — Canada, the Federal Republic of Germany, France and the United Kingdom — three of which are, in fact, comparative studies within the same country. The Canadian and German studies each examine the policies of three separate jurisdictions within a Federal structure (respectively, the provinces of Manitoba, New Brunswick and Ontario; the *Länder* of Bavaria, Berlin and North Rhine-Westphalia); the United Kingdom deals with two populations, the indigenous Welsh-speaking population of Wales and the children of persons who have immigrated to England and Wales, reporting the findings of case studies in four separate areas of the country: Bradford,

	General Treatment	*Detailed Treatment*
Norway	Special language groups (including Lapps/Samit)	
Portugal	Portuguese workers abroad	
Sweden	Nomadic Lapps/Samit Estonians Finnish-speaking and English-speaking Gypsies Immigrants	Immigrants
Switzerland	Immigrants and foreign- language children Romansch-speaking	Immigrants and foreign- language children Romansch-speaking (Graubünden Canton)
Turkey	Turkish workers abroad	Turkish workers abroad
United States	Bilingual education students Native Americans	Bilingual education students

Note: In the table, "immigrants" may refer to children born in the country to persons who have immigrated recently or to descendants of immigrants of earlier generations. National usage varies considerably. Some treated as "immigrants" are, strictly speaking, foreign workers living with special permits.

Coventry, the Inner London Education Authority and Wales. Including France as a single element, an analytical table of studies (Table 2) shows the comparative examination of eleven separate educational jurisdictions in the four country studies. The populations examined have one major commonality. Their life and culture place them clearly in the economic sphere of "Western" industrial society — whether they be established populations such as the Welsh or the Francophones of Canada, or relatively recent immigrants to France, the Federal Republic of Germany and the United Kingdom.

By contrast, the second component (B.) deals with a very different type of population. The common characteristic is that the groups are much less integrated into modern industrial society, and the cultural heritage may depend, at least in part, upon non-integration into that society. These are

TABLE 2 *Minority groups and political jurisdictions treated in the papers of series III*

Case Study	Minority Group	Jurisdiction
A. Linguistic Minorities		
Canada	Francophones	Manitoba New Brunswick Ontario
France	Immigrant and foreign workers	
Germany	German resettlers Immigrant and foreign workers	Bavaria Berlin North Rhine-Westphalia
United Kingdom	Welsh immigrants	Wales Bradford Coventry Inner London
B. Indigenous Cultural Minorities		
Analytical Framework	General Applicability	– – –
Responses to Analytical Framework	Aborigines	Australia
	Lapps/Samit	Norway, Sweden, Finland
	Maoris and Pacific Islanders	New Zealand
	Native American Peoples	Canada, United States

the so-called "indigenous" peoples – Lapps (or Samit) in Scandinavia, Maoris and Pacific Islanders in New Zealand, Aborigines and Torre Strait Islanders in Australia, and North American Indians, Aleuts, and Inuit in Canada and the United States. In this case, the purpose is not so much to describe policies and their effects, as to raise the types of issues that should be considered in later studies of policy. Professor Frank Darnell provided a general statement of issues; this statement was then sent to persons with personal knowledge of the topic (often as a member by ancestry of one of the indigenous populations) who were asked to provide reactions pertinent to their own environment and experience. Even though these responses do not include an outline of policy resembling the case studies (with the partial exception of the paper concerning Maoris and Pacific Islanders), the relevant country mapping studies in Series I provide useful background information to aid in interpretation.

A look at the diversity of the national case studies

Since many readers of this book are likely to come from backgrounds which do not include a broad grounding in comparative education or educational administration, it may be useful to dwell momentarily on the case studies of linguistic minorities and use them to illustrate the diversity of situations found across the broad range of OECD countries studied. Under each of a few major headings we will provide a few general remarks, which do not purport to summarize the vast wealth of detail in the case studies.

Central-local administrative links

In Germany, elementary and secondary education are primarily the responsibility of the states, or *Länder*; in turn, the operation of schools is under control of localities. The margin of discretion of the latter is severely limited by supervision from the *Länder*. Central leadership is provided by a Council of Ministers of Education. By contrast, the French system is much more centralized, with common curricula and examination procedures applying to the entire country. Localities contribute to the upkeep of schools and can influence programme offerings but have little autonomy. The system in England is based upon the delivery of services through local authorities charged with delivery of a broad range of social services; local education authorities are subordinate to these bodies. Little or no direct control over education is exercised by the central government, though the role of the central inspectorate is pervasive, if sometimes difficult to pinpoint. The Canadian model is based upon a federal system that forbids the central government from direct intervention in education, each province having total and exclusive control over the operation of its own system. The three provinces studied all give the operation of schools over to local authorities controlled by elected trustees. Each province has its own province-wide curriculum which all authorities are expected to apply with local adaptations. The degree of local control is highly variable, particularly in relation to finance. Interestingly since the mid-1960s, the Canadian central government has played a major leadership role in stimulating the development of educational services for the French-language minorities of the dominantly English-speaking provinces and of the English minority in Quebec: the exceptional nature of this role stands apart from federal government practice in all other fields related to elementary and secondary schooling.

Minorities discussed

The French and Canadian case studies both focus on a single minority group, the Canadian on minority Francophones in three provinces, the French on children of resident foreign workers. The former therefore overlooks the large group of first and second generation immigrants as well as indigenous peoples; the latter does not treat the problems of France's regional minorities or the populations of its overseas territories. The study of England and Wales deals separately with the Welsh-speaking minority and first and second-generation immigrants (sometimes third generation); it does not include minorities of territories under British control nor, except for an occasional allusion to the Irish, persons resident in England with variant dialects (other than immigrants).

While overlooking many traditional regional minorities such as Danish-speakers, the German study raises the problems of two groups: resident foreign workers and so-called "late resettlers" (*Spätaussiedler*). The latter group, of whose educational problems little is known, is composed of German-speaking persons and others of German descent who have returned to the Federal Republic from countries in Eastern Europe, usually under the terms of bilateral treaties; the term refers mainly to the most recent group of such settlers, those coming since the late 1960s, whose children may have very limited knowledge of German and little preparation for living in West German society.

Financial arrangements

France and Germany fund directly most local salary costs for education (i.e. the central ministry in France and the *Länder* in Germany) with the localities providing contributions to other costs. In England central government subsidies go to local public authorities, not to local education authorities; budgets for schools are in direct competition with monies for other local services such as garbage collection, housing or health care. The Canadian provinces display the whole range of approaches: direct central financing for most operating costs in New Brunswick, a "formula grant" based on complicated weightings of pupil enrolments in relation to factors for local tax-raising capacity in Ontario, and a so-called "foundation" grant system (based on a concept of subsidies to provide a minimum or foundation level of services through all local authorities) in Manitoba. The financing methods for meeting the needs of the minorities cut across all these systems with a complexity that defies summary and is best left for discussion in the appropriate chapters of this book. One interesting detail should be pointed out, however, as it conflicts with almost all standard educational financial practice used in OECD countries until recently: this is the practice that has developed in a number of Western European countries of seeking bilateral arrangements with the governments of countries from which resident foreign workers are drawn. Under such agreements it is typical that the foreign government provides its own nationals as teachers and pays for them: this may be either for a few hours of language instruction or for much larger components of educational time, depending upon the specific arrangements.

Many of the central problems of this study derive from the interplay of factors such as those sketched above. For example, in almost all countries a central concern of policy making is to find the appropriate balance between the powers and functions of central and local or regional educational authorities. Depending upon these arrangements, the type of education offered to minorities may vary significantly. Similarly a central problem of educational finance theory is to determine how different degrees of direct control over expenditures may affect schooling in localities (obviously, a matter to be studied in relationship to a variety of other contributory factors). As we shall see, this study advances relatively strongly-based conclusions about the way in which local autonomy relates to provisions for minority education, and it draws a direct relationship between the degree of central control over subsidies for minority education and the actual delivery of services to the target populations they are intended to benefit. In turn, the different types of minorities, their different characteristics and their relationship to traditional national value systems are a powerful factor in influencing how administrative and financial arrangements affect the quality of services enjoyed by their children.

The issues

The policy issues in this study are best understood in relationship to the previous project on primary schools. It revealed that the financing arrangements developed in the OECD countries studied could be grouped around four major policy goals (see Noah & Sherman, 1979: 6):

(i) Reducing the disparities across and between localities with respect to resources for schooling — termed here the goal of *equality* or equalization.

(ii) Improving the extent to which sub-groups with special needs have access to supplementary resources — termed here the goal of *equity*.

(iii) Encouraging moves to shift the *locus of control* over schooling decisions. Often this has meant strengthening claims by localities that their prerogatives be guarded and/or enhanced — the goal of local autonomy. In other countries the policies emphasis has been on strengthening the hand of other than local authorities to steer school policies.

(iv) Preserving and/or increasing the extent to which parents feel that they have real, practicable opportunities to choose among different styles of schooling for their children — the goal of *diversity and choice*.

The present study arose out of this experience and was shaped by some of the lessons learned (see Noah & Sherman, 1979: 8, 66, 69):

(i) The narrower focus of the earlier study on financial arrangements raised questions such as the extent to which countries use other means, such as regulation, in combination with financial measures to effect policy. Similarly, it was felt that the interpretation of various measures required that they be put into a larger organizational context.

(ii) Difficulties of analysis were traced in part to the diversity of policies treated in the case studies. Grasping the essence of different approaches to the same policy issue would be facilitated by a "common structure focussing directly on a given policy issue and on the range of financial and regulatory devices used in connection with it".

(iii) Finally, the study concluded that it would not be reasonable to pursue conclusions aimed at universal rules applicable to all systems independently of context: "... search for a 'perfect' or 'ideal' system of school finance is likely to be not only unnecessary, but futile. The very variety of school financing arrangements that is observed leads to a strong suspicion that there can be no best way to organize these matters ... some of the important goals set for a school finance system are likely to be mutually inconsistent."

Obviously, since many of the same countries are represented in both studies, the major policy goals of primary school finance systems remain in effect. Emphasis is shifted, nevertheless, to the second item on the list, equity, that is providing supplementary resources to sub-groups with special needs. The Series III papers reveal, however, an interesting fact: the choice of a single population type, linguistic and cultural minorities, did not produce a narrow focus around the educational policy issue of equity. Policy makers have approached these populations with widely divergent goals and have dealt, therefore, with quite divergent issues: attempting to "integrate" a minority group into a system is diametrically opposed to attempting to foster its separateness. Even if the two goals are part of a continuum, they are sufficiently contradictory to lead to very different methods of envisaging the development of policy and its implementation.

To what extent, then, do the policy issues affecting linguistic and cultural minorities overlap with those dealt with in the study of primary school finance? The main overlap concerns the specifics of financial arrangements and the related policy issues. The inherent contradiction in the pursuit of equity and equalization, for example, is always present, and one finds the same range of related policy concerns. On the other hand, the emphasis on an identifiable population or sub-group transforms radically the conceptualization of the policy problem. To the extent that the group is conscious of an identity and has the *potential* of affecting the political environment (actual utilization of voting power may not always be important), the boundaries of the problem open up. Faced with a population whose goals may be different from the assumed goals of the "majority" society, one must confront *de novo* all the issues, even the most fundamental, of what education is all about. In some environments, linguistic and cultural minorities present the first major challenge in modern times to the assumptions underlying the educational system. In short, the overlap between the two studies is mainly at the level of detail such as specifics of financial mechanisms or at the level of broad generalizations such as the relationship of equity and equalization. The minority issue is so powerful, emotionally and socially, that the policy-making ground-rules are transformed; the present study opens up entirely new perspectives of policy development.

A more fruitful avenue of approach may be to point out that linguistic and cultural minorities have a range of concerns that are specific and depart from those of other special populations. As the term used implies, they are a "minority" in the political and social sense within a majority society. The case studies provide extensive proof of how crucial is the relationship minority-majority. This means that the treatment of educational issues is often impossible without reference to the environment outside the school, specifically the degree of integration of the minority within the larger community. Moreover, even if minorities typically share some of the disadvantages associated with certain groups like the handicapped, such as difficulties in reaching the more advanced levels of the educational system, the nature and treatment of the problem cannot be assumed to be the same.

The overriding issues inherent in the discussion of the special educational measures for linguistic and cultural minorities are threefold:

(i) To what extent do the special educational needs of the minority(ies) derive from their distinctive linguistic and cultural characteristics, rather than from characteristics shared with other parts of the general population? Certain linguistic minorities are poor and have educational problems linked to their socio-economic status; measures to further the socio-economic well-being of a larger group of disadvantaged persons might be more appropriate in such a case, than intervention based on ethnicity and language. Conversely in some countries, because of social barriers based on ethnicity and language, any general-impact programme to assist the population as a whole would not significantly improve the lot of the linguistic/cultural minority group.

(ii) To what extent are measures intended to ensure better educational results for a minority consistent with the survival of the minority? In all societies, minorities have begun to question whether "success" in the larger national community must be bought at the expense of the disappearance of their own group and its unique characteristics. On the other hand, most groups recognize the need for a middle ground, and in particular seek to find mechanisms that permit them to benefit from economic advantages of the existing social system without giving up their cultural and linguistic identity.

(iii) To what extent are special measures to help a minority — measures implying usually a recognition of separateness and "difference" from the national majority — compatible with the smooth functioning of the larger society and acceptable to the "majority"? The degree of tolerance for cultural and linguistic differences appears to vary markedly from country to country, though the case studies indicate a growing willingness to accommodate such differences in the schools.

These issues do not call for a single answer. Rather they are issues both of principle and practice that underlie most policy-making debates in the countries studied.

Scope and limitations

The major limitations of the study of linguistic and cultural minorities derive from the newness of comparative studies involving this level of detail with respect to administrative and financial operations. Most comparative education studies are concerned with broad outlines of curriculum content or administrative structures so that this and the predecessor study of primary school finance represent relatively new departures. Unresolved difficulties remain in reconciling the vocabulary and approach of case studies framed in different national settings. Despite the quite detailed specifications provided for the case studies (for both Series I and Series III), the great differences in emphasis and tradition between countries have resulted in corresponding differences in the information presented. As a result, this analysis must be taken as a first cursory attempt to look across a broad spectrum of information to define common elements and trends. Because case studies are rarely conclusive and inevitably reflect the views of the individual author, the conclusions derived here are subject to careful re-evaluation and further study. Even where this review succeeds in interpreting correctly the views of a case study author, it is not only possible but highly probable that the author's views on many points would be contested by other well-informed persons within his or her country.

Certain limitations are also imposed by the specification of the study framework. Two are particularly worth mention. The concept of a "minority" is extremely difficult to define in terms which are meaningful in a social sense. This is patently obvious in the case of certain multi-linguistic, multi-cultural states. Switzerland is an example of a nation within which three groups speaking a major language (French, German, Italian) and one minor group (Romansch) coexist on a basis which makes it difficult to speak of a "minority" or a "majority" in the same sense as elsewhere. In Belgium (not included in this series of studies) the numerical boundary between language minority and language majority has shifted within living memory. In Canada the Francophones constitute minorities in nine provinces but are a majority in the tenth (Québec); certain Québec writers refer to a "double minority, double majority" to categorize the situation. In Spain the recent recognition of regional aspirations leaves a situation where, despite the centuries-old dominance of the Castilian language, those speaking regional languages (usually in addition to Castilian) are usually a clear majority in their own region but where no single group, in strict numerical terms, constitutes a unified majority across the country. The difficulties of definitions result less from the specifications of the project than from the nature of sociolinguistic phenomena: the concept of numerical majority is not always synonymous with a dominant political and social position, and membership in a given linguistic and cultural group often is uncertain for the individuals concerned. This ambiguity of the words "minority" and "majority" should be kept in mind throughout the following discussion.

A second limitation derives from the project specifications. In the absence of a rigorous set of definitions, authors were given freedom in deciding what would be treated as "organizational" and "governance" measures. Usually there is no ambiguity in dealing with the paper of a given author, but the variety of usage across countries obliges us to define here a few terms. The remainder of this analysis can be understood fully without fully assimilating all the distinctions given in this section, to which reference may be made when required. Hurried readers are advised to skim it rapidly.

Authors have sometimes failed to distinguish between: (a) descriptions of how educational systems and their governance are organized and operate at a given moment, and (b) the discussion of policy measures or options that change the existing system and its principles of operation. In the following, "organization" will be dealt with in two contexts:

(i) *Organizational arrangements* existing at a given time. One may distinguish between: (a) the administrative framework for organizing school experiences (the network of hierarchical relationships between persons and institutions commonly shown on organization charts); (b) provisions for instruction, comprising the main elements of organizing the curriculum (content of courses, uses of languages for instruction, grouping of students, allocation of time in the school programme, general sequence of courses (cf. curriculum levels specified by Marklund cited in Maclure, 1972:12); and (c) support or ancillary services rendering assistance to students or teachers outside the classroom situation (psychological testing or referral services, school transport, social assistance to families, curriculum centres for teachers, etc).

(ii) *Organizational changes or "instruments"*; A change in existing organizational arrangements made to effect a given policy objective.

The absence of a definition for "governance" led to its use in the papers with two meanings. A restricted view of governance sees the structure of policy making and administration as a fixed entity that is part of the

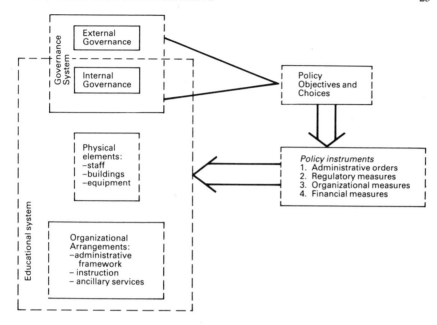

FIGURE 1   *Policy instruments in relation to components of the governance system and the educational system*

educational system. Given general policy goals, this governance structure chooses the appropriate combination of measures to attain the goals. For example, a study may note that, in addition to financial incentives, the authorities decided to use mandatory regulations to ensure that a certain type of instruction was provided to a minority. This view sees governance in terms of its role within the educational system, a concept we shall call *internal governance*. A larger view sees the educational system as one component in a larger policy making system, one public sector among several. The educational system itself, including the role of different participants in the governance system, is subject to being changed. The concept of *external governance* includes consideration of external factors that determine policy choices, such as the role of different public groups in political life.

The "internal" view dominates in the papers in Series I and is consistent with the technical viewpoint usually adopted to describe educational measures for groups such as the handicapped. The studies for Series III, however, take a broader view and describe issues such as the role of linguistic and cultural minorities in the political process and the extent they are allowed to participate in the (external) governance process. No author has adopted a strict definition of governance, and in the discussions that follow it is necessary to keep both meanings of the term in mind.

In addition to the distinction between internal and external governance, the following vocabulary will be used:

(i) *The governance system* comprises all the elements (persons, organisms, processes) of the *decision-making* system involved in the conception, development, formulation, and adoption of policy, as well as the *administrative execution and control* system for interpreting, applying and ensuring adherence to policy. Some persons or organisms (e.g. senior educational administrators) participate both in decision-making on policy and in administration.

(ii) *Governance measures or "instruments"* are acts of an administrative or regulatory nature taken to carry out a policy objective. Four kinds of measure may be distinguished: (a) *Administrative orders* are directives addressed from superiors to subordinates requiring the taking of specific acts of an individual nature. Such measures are not discussed in the studies and are not further dealt with here. (b) *Regulatory measures* are directives having general, rather than individual, applicability. The legal status of the measures may vary widely. Examples include: "regulations", "circulars", "memoranda", "guidelines", and "recommendations". (c) *Organizational measures* are exactly the same as the organizational changes defined earlier, that is modifications to the existing organization of education for the purpose of implementing a policy. (d) *Financial measures* are steps taken to control the flow of resources into different parts of the educational system and may involve either control of monetary flows or the provision of real resources (such as teachers or equipment).

These distinctions help clarify the purpose of the project as a whole, to study the way policy-makers choose different policy instruments and the consequences of their choices. For the purposes of this analysis, a *policy instrument* is any formal means adopted to define and put into practice a given set of educational objectives. For a given policy, four types of instrument are available: administrative orders, organizational changes, regulatory measures (termed "governance" measures in some studies), and financial measures. Options are exercised between different instruments within the governance system, which is also responsible for the administrative execution of the policy within the framework defined by the instruments.

The policy making and implementation process

The original specifications for the case studies of language minority groups consisted of a description of major types of information to be presented by the authors (Table 3). To facilitate analysis of the resulting studies and the comparison of policy actions, a simple model was prepared to show the inter-relationship between the major topics on which informa-

TABLE 3   *Structure of national case studies of linguistic and cultural minorities*

I.   Introduction

II. Background
     A. History and Identification of Cultural Groups
     B. Particular Cultural Groups: Aspirations
     C. The Role of Language and Literacy
     D. History of Language and Literacy Policy with particular reference to formal education

III. Language and Literacy Policy for Education in a Multicultural Society
     A. Language and Literacy Policy for the Particular Groups Studied
         1. Objectives – implicit and explicit
         2. Legal status
         3. Financial arrangements – source, type, form
         4. Organisational structures
         5. Governance procedures

IV. B. Overview of the Provisions
         1. Inherent strengths and weaknesses
         2. Role of financial arrangements
         3. Adaptability of organisational and administrative procedures to changing needs
         4. Effectiveness of financial, organisational and governance arrangements

V.   Conclusions and areas for international comparison

Adapted from Brief for Country Experts

tion was provided (Figure 2). By comparison with the guidelines for authors, it includes certain new or unspecified elements: (i) recognition of public support as a key element in policy making and implementation; (ii) separation of governance into its internal and external elements; (iii) showing changes to the governance system itself as one type of policy instrument; (iv) showing three elements of the educational delivery system on which organizational, regulatory, and financial instruments have an impact, namely the administrative framework, specific provisions for instruction, and support and ancillary services.

The topics presented in the model have been grouped as follows for purposes of the discussion in this report:

(i) *Minority group characteristics*: Most authors agree on the major pertinent factors, such as absolute and relative size of the group, territorial concentration, degree of maintenance of the language and culture, recency of settlement and so forth.

(ii) *National background factors*: The factors include levels of governance (both for general policy and for education), national administrative tradition, traditions regarding language and literacy along with any recent evolution in these, and the stage of development of educational provision for the minority.

(iii) *Policy objectives and public support*: Official policy objectives are treated in relation to the objectives of the minority(ies) and the dominant trends in public support for policies.

(iv) *Legal status and framework*: The choice of policy instruments in terms of their legal nature depends in part upon background factors such as national administrative tradition. But the choice itself is often important for symbolic as well as practical reasons. Although not usually discussed in this light, the legal status of the minority group is both a background factor of the governance process (narrowly defined) and a *result* of the same process (broadly defined).

(v) *Organizational arrangements* are discussed under three main headings: (a) the administrative framework, including both the general hierarchy of supervision and the system of grouping students in classes, programmes and schools, (b) the provisions for instruction, including the role of the minority and majority languages, curriculum content and special dispositions for instructional grouping; (c) support and ancillary services both for classroom instruction and for the training of teachers and classroom aides.

(vi) *Financial instruments*: Financial arrangements are discussed in terms of their relationship to the issues of equalization and equity,

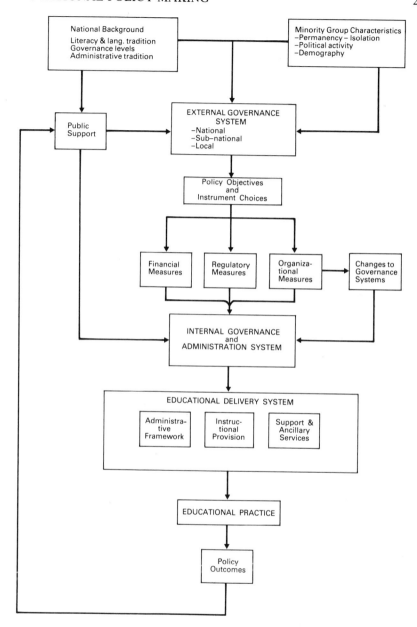

FIGURE 2   *A model of the Relationship between elements and factors analysed in the study*

the role of incentives particularly in multi-level governance systems, the place of direct finance of special programmes and the major factors governing the choice of instruments.

(vii) *Governance*: The discussion deals primarily with the broader definition of governance, in particular the relationship between minorities and the governance system.

(viii) *Educational practice*: What goes on in classrooms is directly affected by all of the elements mentioned thus far. However, the classroom itself has its own internal rules of operation and assumptions, many of which operate independently from the administrative and governance structure to which it is subordinated. Teachers and students bring to the classroom their own structure of expectations, leading to operative characteristics of education which are the *de facto* policy seen by the minority language students. Lack of systematic information makes it impossible to devote a special section to this topic, which is nevertheless treated in several contexts.

(ix) *Rationale for policy making*: Rationales may be considered the underlying assumptions used in articulating policy objectives and instruments. (The term is often used simply to refer to whatever objectives and justification are acknowledged formally as the basis of a policy; the use in this analysis includes implicit as well as explicit rationales.)

The major questions: Objectives, policy instruments and educational practice

The purpose of this analysis is to use the background information provided in the different studies as a means of answering the following questions:

(i) What are the major factors that affect the development and implementation of policy related to the education of linguistic and cultural minorities in the OECD countries?

(ii) What types of policy instrument are used by authorities and what difference does the choice of one or another instrument make to the educational provision made for the minorities?

(iii) What are the different modes of organizing the educational provision in terms of content (linguistic or otherwise), administrative framework, and support services? What are the major implications of the choice of modes and what factors determine the choices made?

(iv) How do the elements of finance, organization and governance relate to each other and to the general issue of the extent to which the minority group exercises control over, or influence on, the education offered to its members?

Even a most perfunctory examination of the list of questions shows that definitive answers are probably not possible on the basis of this (or any other) set of studies. Too many value judgements would underlie the responses to be given, even if all the studies were extremely complete as to detail. The answers given to these questions should be construed as working hypotheses rather than definitive responses. The value of the study lies in the fact that, heretofore, few of the hypotheses could have been formulated with any degree of specificity or in the knowledge that they were relevant to the educational systems of the countries involved.

Notes to Chapter 2

1. The following countries have membership or associate status in the Organisation for Economic Co-operation and Development: Australia, Austria, Belgium, Canada, Denmark, Finland, France, (Federal Republic of) Germany, Greece, Iceland, Ireland, Italy, Japan, Luxembourg, The Netherlands, New Zealand, Norway, Portugal, Spain, Sweden, Switzerland, Turkey, United Kingdom, United States of America, Yugoslavia.
2. In all of the matters under discussion, Sweden has pursued policies for several years that are more favourable to the interests of the foreign workers than those of any other jurisdiction.

3 Public support and the definition of policy objectives

Policy making related to the education of linguistic and cultural minorities is embedded in a political and social context that extends far beyond the present educational system of a jurisdiction. On the one hand, there is an important accretion of factors to be taken into account whose nature is the product of history: these background factors include both the characteristics of the minority group, or groups, concerned and the history of language and literacy policy in the country. On the other hand, there are the human actors involved in the policy making processes either as participants or potential beneficiaries of the policies made. The setting of educational objectives for minority groups involves three sets of actors, whose objectives may be mutually contradictory: educators and others who are currently employed in the management and operation of the educational system, the general public — the "majority" group in each context — whose attitudes constitute the national (or regional) climate of opinion, and the members of the minority group(s). In considering these actors, the main issue for analysis is not their objectives at a given point in time but rather the factors that shape and change the objectives, as well as the way the objectives of different groups interact.

The case studies document the crucial role of public attitudes and support in shaping the objectives of education for linguistic and cultural minorities. This influence is reflected not only through the political process of educational governance but also (and perhaps with greater force) through the implicit definitions of educational problems that are the basis for developing policy objectives. Minority education is somewhat different from certain other areas of educational policy. Many day-to-day decisions about the operation of educational systems may be dealt with as educational problems in a narrow "technical" sense, that is as matters for decision by well-informed professional educators, with little need for consultation outside the educational system except with those most directly affected: individual students, their parents or, occasionally, organized groups of parents. At least in the recent past, most jurisdictions have ceased dealing with minority education on a simply "technical" basis. Coping with the needs of linguistic and cultural groups outside the majority group in a given jurisdiction often poses a serious threat to the *status quo* both of school practice and public attitudes to education. The interaction between background factors and the attitudes of different participants in the policy process is highly complex but, in all instances, public attitudes and support appear to be crucial for the successful implementation of any line of policy adopted. Little is possible unless there is a minimum of consensus between educators, the general public, and the members of the minority(ies).

Background factors

Minority group characteristics

Public policies on linguistic and cultural minorities are responsive in the first instance to the characteristics of the minorities concerned. The most important differences between minorities derive from raw demographic facts: absolute numbers, concentration in given areas, relative numbers as part of the total population and recency of settlement in their home area(s). A second set of differences is essentially socio-cultural. It concerns generally the way the members of the minority relate to each other, to their own linguistic and cultural tradition, and to the majority society. Policy makers must cope with a range of population needs that contrasts with the relatively even distribution of other types of special populations (e.g. the deaf, the blind, the retarded) across different countries. One might note the difference in demands placed upon a country such as Canada, where one minority language group of several million members is concentrated, for the most part, in the single province of Quebec, with those that are generated by a relative handful of political refugees from Southeast Asia in a country such as Sweden. Or, in socio-cultural terms, one can cite the difference between the case of immigrants who arrive in some countris with the firm intention of becoming members of its society and integrating with it, and the case of certain groups who have been known to stick obstinately to their language, religion, and cultural traditions with unremitting persistence over generations (the overseas Chinese of the Pacific perimeter being perhaps the best known, though many parallel examples are found in the OECD countries). Between these extremes are to be found most of the minorities under study, groups whose members hesitate between identification with their minority role and with the majority society, who practice a form of bilingualism in which two languages alternate in different environments with neither being completely native-like, and whose cultural roots are an eclectic selection of elements of religion, family relationship practices, lifestyle, and folkloric traditions.

The individual case studies provide background information on the groups treated but usually do not attempt to derive specific "rules" or principles about the relationship between population characteristics and public policy responses to their needs. It is only at a certain level of detail within each national context that the relationships are treated. Thus, within a given country, one can note the obvious, for example that education provision for minorities usually exists in areas where the minorities are concentrated, as in the United Kingdom where funds are channelled to cities where large immigrant populations are established. The Canadian study provides a somewhat similar example, where the relative degree of control of Francophones over their education appears to vary from province to province as a function of population density and concentration, though not as a function necessarily of absolute size: the New Brunswick Francophones enjoy greater control of their schools than the much larger concentration of Franco-Ontarians, in part because they form a much larger proportion of the population of their province and in part because they are very highly concentrated in some areas.

Such generalizations are much more difficult *across* national situations, simply because so many other factors intervene along with the characteristics of the minority population. Thus one may contrast the almost total exclusion from the political process of millions of resident foreign workers in several European countries with the administrative autonomy of the minute Romansch population in one canton of Switzerland. In dealing with the studies as a whole, the main point to keep in mind is the extreme diversity of situations across Member countries and, within countries, between regions and even between minorities. With this in mind, we can recall a few of the dimensions of this diversity and the way it interacts with policy:

Length of establishment

The populations fall into three categories. The indigenous peoples are, by and large, the longest established, even if they have often been pushed back from their ancestral territories, the Lapps ever further northwards, the American Indians into reservations, and the Australian aborigines in some of the least hospitable areas of the continent. Most countries have "established" minorities whose presence predates the period when the modern nation-state took shape — the Welsh in the United Kingdom, the constituent peoples of the Helvetic confederation, the Catalonians in Spain or, for the newer countries of America, the Spanish-speakers of the U.S. Southwest and the Francophones of Canada. The newest group is the result of different waves of European migration, some dating back more than a century but most of it from the period since World War II. By and large, the established minorities are those whose concerns for educational provision are most likely to be dealt with as a matter of "rights" rather than as a transitory set of measures destined to palliate temporary social disadvantage. Only the established minorities can lay claim to a right to conserve their identity and can back it with political might. Despite their greater antiquity, the indigenous peoples are rarely in a position to assert their claims in ways that affect elections and ballot boxes, though the Response Paper by Dammert as well as the U.S. mapping study, indicate that, at least in some parts of North America, this situation may be changing.

Geographic isolation

Geographic isolation is a factor in development of educational policy mainly for indigenous peoples. Such isolation may be viewed as a benefit if the result is to reduce the negative effects of contacts with the mainstream culture of the country involved, or as a disadvantage if it tends to reinforce a socially disadvantaged status. The Norwegian mapping study illustrates a case where vigorous financial and other measures have been applied to foster geographical equality of access to education; though not directed to a specific linguistic or cultural minority, the policy helps Lappish/Samit populations along with others in the same areas. Sweden and Australia, on the other hand, have adopted specific measures inspired by problems of isolation but have linked them with programmes aimed at specific indige-nous populations (Aborigines and Lapps/Samit).

Cultural isolation

Isolation may be a social phenomenon. Ghettoization is primarily linked to groups that have inferior social status (in the eyes of the surrounding population). The case studies of Germany, France and the United King-dom, all illustrate specific examples of groups having difficulty integrating into, or even establishing contact with, the surrounding society. Such a situation, as for example in the case of resident foreign workers and their children, may so reduce the opportunities for use of the language of the host country that it counteracts the effects of language training classes. On the other hand, it also reveals the crucial importance of the school experience, which for many children in such situations, is the *only* place where they have contact with native citizens of the country. As the German report notes, immigrant groups may shun contact with immigrants from other countries. The so-called "Bavarian model" of school, in which non-German students are grouped together for instruction during most of their studies, shows the delicate tradeoffs that must be weighed in decision-making: isolation will tend to reinforce the use of the home language of the children but conversely decreases their chances of direct contact with Germans and the German language. Such an effect is consistent with the objective of eventual return of the children to the homeland of their parents but may reduce their freedom of choice with respect to remaining in the new host country.

Geographic "containedness"

The concentration of a given ethnic or cultural group in a bounded geographic area may encourage the recognition of their needs and the provision of relevant services, quite independently of the total numbers involved. In some of the OECD countries (e.g. Belgium, Canada, Finland, Spain) the areas involved may represent a significant portion of the total national territory and population. The main problem noted in the studies is that of the larger urban areas where very significant immigrant or foreign workers populations may live on a dispersed basis, thus facing authorities with difficult choices with regard to schooling. Having 25 pupils of one nationality in a school at a given age level makes it possible easily to create special classes; having twice that number split into six nationalities calls for other measures. As noted in a recent Swedish official circular, the pedagogical advantages of bringing pupils of one nationality together in a central place must be weighed against numerous potential disadvantages: greater distances to travel to school, loss of contact between pupils and other children of same age living in their own area, creation of "immigrant schools", and difficulty for parents to remain in contact with the school (Skolöverstyrelsen, May 1979). Geographic containedness has been a very important positive factor, in that for stable, established minorities it may be the key to long-term survival (cf. Danish areas of Sleswig-Holstein, Valle d'Aosta in Italy, Åland Archipelago in Finland).

Political awareness and participation

Provision of special services for a linguistic or cultural minority is seldom a politically neutral act in the eyes of the majority population. The recognition of the need for such services, a first step towards their provision, may depend upon the ability of the minorities concerned to use political power effectively. Access to such power is dependent, in most cases, upon the legal status and history of the group(s) concerned. Whereas the "established" minorities have, by and large, political rights, the resident foreign workers of Western Europe usually have little, or no, right to participation in the political life of their countries of residence; the result has been, in many cases, a very delayed reaction to their needs on the part of the relevant national authorities. The history of arrangements for these groups shows, in a number of cases, the role played by the authorities of their countries of origin, i.e. the countries where they do potentially have political rights. The series of bilateral arrangements between authorities in France and Germany with their counterparts in the countries of emigration show how political actions at the international level can supplement the almost non-existent political strength of such groups.

Demography

As mentioned earlier, raw numbers count. The reaction to a given minority depends often upon simple demographic evolution: a group perceived to be numerous and continuing to increase in size is likely to be able to attract attention from the public and policy makers because its members are expected to be a long-term feature of society; they are likely to be dealt with more positively than persons from a group perceived to be temporary, whether because the group is declining in absolute numbers through emigration or because assimilation into the majority causes it to lose its separate identity. Turning from the political level to that of educational practice, a multitude of decisions regarding services are directly linked to numbers of pupils, their concentration, permanency and so forth. The major difficulty with demographic data is that they are not absolute: each national situation interprets numbers in widely differing ways. Norwegian educators have been known to point out that a typical secondary school in Norway would be considered too small to be viable in some other countries. The case studies do provide, however, one exception that confirms, so to speak, the rule: the decision in Switzerland to create the canton of Graubünden was taken largely because of the perception that, without it, the Romansch language groups would shortly disappear. Where educational (or other social) provision is linked to numbers in some direct fashion, demographic data can be at the centre of controversy, with different groups disagreeing about the basic "facts" in a situation.

National background factors

The nature of the response made to the educational needs of minorities
is as varied as the countries studied. The interest of the comparison
between countries resides less in the differences of their national histories
than in the commonalities of the forces operating as their very different
systems come to grips with common problems. At this point, we shall
summarize the main groupings of characteristics identified (particularly in
the case studies of Series III) and describe a few of the forces that shape the
policy making process.

History of attitudes to languages and literacy
The case studies detail the specifics of each country's individual evolution as regards its treatment of minority languages. Despite widely
differing histories, all countries shared in the common concerns of the
Nineteenth Century: the spread of public educational systems was part of
an historical pattern in which all adopted a certain minimum of linguistic
uniformity; the decisions taken in setting up public education in the 1800s
were usually based upon and tended to reinforce earlier patterns of
subordination for less powerful groups. The proscription of the Welsh
language from the schools in 1870 was simply a confirmation of the
dominance of English in the United Kingdom which dated back for
centuries in other state-controlled activities, such as the courts of law.
Legal recognition of more than one official language has been reserved to
those rare states where the balance of power between the different groups
was such that none established permanent ascendancy over the other (cf.
Belgium, Canada, Switzerland). Most of the countries studied, followed
the Nineteenth Century trend of adopting a single, dominant dialect of
each official language as a basis for instruction, despite the variety of
popular speech. The crucial issue for this study is how the great majority of
countries have come within the last few decades to a situation where
historical patterns of uniformity have been relaxed; the extent of relaxation
varies, of course, but the trend is well-nigh universal. The pattern in each
country is unique: in response to one force or another (large-scale
settlement in France and Germany, serious problems in schools in major
United Kingdom centres, political mobilization among Francophones in
Canada) adaptations are being made. However, the needs of minorities are
not new, nor is the existence of pressures resisting the imposition of
linguistic uniformity. What is new in all cases is the willingness to react.
There appears to be a growing tolerance of diversity in the countries
studied, a phenomenon that transcends national borders and differences.

Despite the overwhelming weight of attachment to unilingual education shared by all countries and, one suspects, the majority of their citizens, all the OECD countries are experimenting with forms of education which permit some degree of use for the mother tongue of minorities. The only study that puts forward an hypothesis regarding this long-term change of opinion that has occurred (Canada) links it to factors of urbanization and continued prosperity after World War II, which contributed to break down traditional structures and attitudes. Little appears to be known about the causes and long-term evolution of opinion across countries, but the case studies provide ample reasons why more research should be done on this topic.

Levels of governance

It may be a truism to point it out, but the policy responses to linguistic and cultural minorities are shaped by the constitutional and legislative arrangements that surround public services in the respective countries. The OECD states run the full gamut from the centralized unitary state (France) through the decentralized unitary state (England) to the partial or complete federation (Australia, Canada, Switzerland, the United States, Yugoslavia); the description of educational arrangements for minorities is, by and large, modelled to respect the existing arrangements. It is interesting to note, however, that in at least some cases, the existence of special populations requiring educational services has provided the impetus for relatively major shifts of practice: the direct intervention of the United States government in elementary and secondary education is a relatively recent phenomenon and was justified politically on the grounds of helping certain disadvantaged repeatedly; the adoption of the 1968 Bilingual Education Act (since amended twice) was merely an extension of this precedent. The measures taken by the Canadian Federal authorities in support of bilingual education represent perhaps an even greater break with tradition, given the very strong resistance of provinces to allow any incursions into the provincial domain of education. The Canadian case studies also illustrate, within the separate provinces, a similar tendency: the more senior level of government may intervene at a lower level in order to protect the interests of a minority (the provinces in the local education authorities). The tendency found in some western European countries, such as France and Germany, to make bilateral arrangements with foreign governments to assist in the training of their own nationals may be explained in part by the necessity of finding some means that go outside the established governance arrangements in order to deal with the special populations concerned.

Administrative traditions

The shape of the provision made for linguistic and cultural minorities appears most to be determined by the traditions of governance and educational administration in each country. There are few, if any, examples, in the case studies or mapping studies where the education of a linguistic or cultural minority has been the cause of a major restructuring of administrative and governance relationships. Policy makers juggle with existing structures but rarely develop responses that are totally new. This does not rule out major reforms. The creation of a canton in Switzerland for the Romansch-speaking population was a governance change that altered the constitutional configuration of the country. Yet this change, which affected all areas of administration and not just education, fit within a long-standing administrative and legislative tradition: a traditional governance structure was extended to provide a new language group with certain protection. The flexibility demonstrated in this respect can be contrasted with the relative inflexibility of the cantonal structures themselves: despite potential advantages for individual mobility of citizens, most of the Swiss cantons stick steadfastly to their rule of one language per territory (but with their well-known flexibility of several languages per *citizen* in many places). The significant intervention by the Canadian government, referred to previously, also bears the imprint of its federal tradition: non-earmarked grants were provided through a system that was negotiated on a multilateral basis with the provinces.

Where educational provision for the minority requires measures going against administrative traditions and structures, progress may be slow or negligible. The urgency of educational problems of minorities in the United Kingdom has not resulted, for example, in the creation of population-specific programmes under central control. Most funds are channelled to local authorities though the Rate Support Grant, and indirect measures of suasion (e.g. the influence of the Inspectorate) are used to favour the minorities. A partial exception to this rule is the provision of Section II grants (Section II, Local Government Act 1966) to help communities with large numbers of immigrants; again, however, the grants are available for the entire range of local services rather than just for education.

The persistence of administrative traditions is not analysed in the case studies, but one can hypothesize the major reasons for it. First and foremost is the general inertia of administrative systems and bureaucracies, too well-known to comment on further. Related to this is a serious technical problem: setting up programmes which are at a variance with "normal administrative procedure" involves making a host of technical changes cutting across the operations of several departments: non-standard financial practices may require, in addition to the amendment of numerous laws and regulations, changes to accounting and auditing procedures as well as the general system of information flow in governmental agencies. The role of such technical problems is hard to overestimate. Finally, even where the political will exists to set up new arrangements going at cross-purposes with administrative tradition, it frequently becomes clear that the tradition is more than the product of the inner workings of an administrative structure; it may represent the outcome of decades (if not centuries) of political compromises, often reflecting major social and political forces far more powerful than the political motives that gave rise to the desire to set up the new programme. Few, if any, major innovations of administrative practice are initiated to serve a single programme. The major changes of financial practice documented in some countries in the earlier study of primary school finance (mainly to foster equalization between different regions or localities) favoured all aspects of education.

Policy objectives from "inside": the educator's view

Since the case studies and mapping studies have been written mainly from the point of view of those who work in, and directly administer, the educational system, they contain little direct reflection on the autonomous role played by administrators and teachers in shaping the *de facto* objectives pursued in schools. The role of national administrative tradition, mentioned above as a background factor, is clearly reflected within the educational system itself. It is closely paralleled by a set of traditional teaching practices of which teachers themselves may hardly be aware. The case studies illustrate, for example, the uniformity of approach to language and dialect in the classroom across most countries until very recently; schools normally operate in only one or, at most, two standard official languages with relatively little "flexing" to the different dialects and social differences in language use found among pupils of different regions or social classes. The assumption that there is a "right" way to speak or write is so deeply ingrained in teaching practice (not to mention testing procedures) for majority group pupils, that it long went unrecognized as a factor in dealing with minority groups. Even where the implications of the assumption are recognized, and positive efforts are made to counter its potentially negative effects, teachers have little room for drastically modifying their practices, unless they also are willing to adopt an entirely new approach to the issue of language and dialect for all groups and unless the whole educational system is involved in the change. As the case study for England and Wales notes: "Multicultural education without multicultural examinations is a contradiction" (Rosen, p. 64).

The example of dialect shows the limits of "technical" changes: a teacher cannot revise the approach to dialect unless this is recognized in the examination and promotion system. Equally the examination and promotion standards are a matter of public concern, and the public opinion of most countries is very unwilling to accept any change that appears to weaken so-called "basic standards". Partially creolized versions of English and French from former colonies are hardly acceptable as media of instruction for public opinion in the United Kingdom and France. It is interesting that, in some cases, it might be much easier to obtain public support for the introduction of a totally different foreign language as a medium of instruction for a portion of the studies of minority groups, than it would be to accept an "incorrect" version of the national language.

This schema places the members of the educational system in a double role. First they are required to make decisions mediating between a variety of factors: policy received from more senior levels, external opinion, needs of individuals, and the nature of the problem at hand. Secondly they are themselves, as individuals, stake-holders in the decisions made. Teachers are strongly concerned in their own right about the nature of the teaching they give, the standards they set, and their sense of what is "right". Furthermore, as groups, educators may be affected directly in their lives by decisions. The case study of Germany gives a particularly good example of this in connection with provision of instruction in the home language of pupils: in Berlin a decision to move in this direction might menace several hundred teaching jobs of existing staff. The Swedish policy of providing specialized pre-service training to teachers who speak Finnish as a means of helping them to deal with minority Finnish-speaking students, thereby sets up a qualification for specialized teachers that could, in some circumstances, provide them with greater choice on the job market. In Canada, decisions to set up separate French-language schools rather than to maintain existing mixed French-English schools can result in serious displacements not only for teachers but also, for example, for school principals, who might see a major part of their responsibilities disappear as a portion of the student body is removed from their control.

The multiplicity of roles played by educators is intrinsically interesting for analysis but, for present purposes, less relevant than the factors that cause them to act in setting and changing objectives. The case studies seem to indicate that, by and large, initiatives from within the educational system are limited to dealing with problems of linguistic and cultural minorities as "technical" issues, i.e. the taking of measures to reduce perceived handicaps of minorities in meeting the *current objectives* of the educational system. The range of measures available appears to be quite limited, unless there is strong backing for change at the political level. A teacher may, for example, provide limited extra assistance in learning German for a group of foreign pupils, but provision of large numbers of extra hours of tuition requires the mobilization of resources, well beyond the limits available at the school or class level. To introduce *new objectives*, such as developing language competence in the language of a minority pupil's home, is even more difficult. Even though teachers are often leaders in providing advice favouring such actions, the case studies show that such far-reaching changes go beyond the "technical" decision-making latitude afforded to educators and, in almost all cases, require political ratification based on at least a minimum consensus of public opinion.

The evolution of public opinion on minorities

The almost universal recognition within OECD countries of the special needs of linguistic and cultural minorities, together with the development of associated educational remedies, bears testimony to a relatively broad public consensus. This consensus represents a massive shift of public priorities and attitudes in the last few decades. The shift is visible both in countries like Canada with long-established minorities and in those that have had to deal with large numbers of recent immigrants or settlers, as in Western Europe. In each case, the majority society has shown a greater willingness than in the past to recognize the special needs of minorities and to search for appropriate solutions to their problems.

A key factor in the greater willingness to deal with minorities has been the growing awareness that they represent an enduring, rather than temporary, problem for educational authorities. For an established minority, such as the Canadian Francophones outside Quebec, public awareness that the groups are not likely to disappear in the short term has made it possible to adopt policies that overtly seek to perpetuate the French language and culture for the indefinite future. In England and Wales the failure of immigrants to assimilate, even in the second generation, has drawn attention to the need for different educational approaches. Countries like France and West Germany have passed through different phases of policy direction, reflecting different assessments of the degree of permanence of the problem. The first phase might be described as virtually ignoring the problem; resident foreign workers were perceived as temporary visitors to the countries involved; whatever problems their children encountered in the educational sphere were assumed to be temporary, of a nature that would solve itself as soon as they returned to their home country. The 1970s in particular appear to have marked a turning point, as western European nations recognized the enduring structural change resulting from the presence in their societies of some 14–15 million foreign workers and dependents, most of whom tended to remain in their new countries of residence. The fact that the so-called "rotation model" (where it was assumed workers would return to their home countries to be replaced by new groups) was no longer viable, has been at the origin of the search for solutions (Rist, 1980). This second phase has resulted in broad public awareness of the problem, but the case studies reveal no indication that a consensus has arisen as to the solutions. The German case study is typical, as it documents the hesitations of the public and authorities in defining objectives for the education provided to the minorities: in some cases (e.g. Berlin) the model assumes that the children should be helped to enter German society, in others (e.g. Bavaria) the emphasis is on preparing them for re-entry to the home societies of their parents.

It is interesting to note that the nature of the problem identified by authorities and public opinion, both in the United Kingdom and in continental Europe, appears to be similar, despite the difference in initial assumptions. In England and Wales the assumption that immigrants would assimilate easily, proved unfounded; in continental Europe, the parallel assumption that workers would "rotate" has also proved fallacious. The passage of time appears to be leading toward a third phase of dealing with immigrants and foreign workers, the recognition that the groups may be a permanent feature of society, groups that are neither immediately "assimilatable" into their new country of residence nor readily adaptable for return to their home countries — a sort of new social class in Western Europe.

The mapping studies also indicate a similar process in countries such as the United States, Australia and New Zealand. In Australia, for example, the 1967 referendum transferring responsibility for education of Aboriginal peoples to the Federal Government, was a milestone in public recognition of the importance of the problem posed by their education. The intractable problems encountered since then in translating public willingness to act, into effective programmes for the Aboriginal peoples, has led to serious questioning, evidenced in the mapping study, of the objectives and modes of such education. This questioning is also apparent in the United States, where the great size of the affected populations and their growing political awareness, are factors to be reckoned with; the student population potentially affected by bilingual programmes in the age group 4–18 years is estimated by the mapping study at some 3.6 million, most of them of Hispanic origin. Whereas most policy is phrased in terms related to helping such students to progress in the regular (English language) system, the fact that many of those affected have maintained their native language through numerous generations and appear unlikely to lose it in the foreseeable future, has pushed United States opinion towards acceptance of the enduring nature of the problem (Leibowitz, 1980). Finally, if one examines the question of education for indigenous peoples in terms of its content, it becomes clear that, even when the matter of home language is removed (many Native American Indians, for example, have lost the knowledge of their ancestral languages), the cultural differences alone have proved sufficient obstacles to the success of education based upon earlier principles of uniformity of treatment.

The enduring nature of the problem posed by such minorities may help to explain the recognition of the problem, but not the willingness being shown to search for solutions that take into account the special needs and desires of the minorities. The following are the factors identifiable from the case studies that appear to have had major influence:

Existence of recognizable educational problems similar to "traditional" problems of special education. Educators are usually extremely sensitive to such problems as they appear in students in schools. Because special education for the handicapped is a common measure available to the majority, taking steps to help individual students cope with learning problems is already legitimated, and public opinion (if the steps become known at all) tends immediately to be receptive to such action. Considerable efforts are required, however, to get public opinion to accept measures aimed at entire groups of students identified by language or ethnicity. Efforts to help a group are considered giving them a special status or privileges.

Internal social pressures felt in the political life of the country involved. Large groups of citizens having social problems (such as the Canadian Francophones, United States Hispanics, Catalans in Spain and Welsh in the United Kingdom) may constitute significant pressure groups and exercise influence through the usual political process, even if they are not in a majority. The resident foreign workers of Western Europe, on the other hand, are almost totally disenfranchised. Political pressures to help them tend, therefore, to be indirect, i.e. exercised by others on their behalf. Disinterested help may come from political groups or individuals acting out of principle, or the stimulus may be self-interested demands by parents from the majority group, whose concern that the level of schooling for their children not be lowered by large numbers of poorly-performing minority children, causes them to lobby for changes to improve the situation.

International intervention and commitments.   The protection of resident foreign workers in the European Economic Community appears to have been favoured by the existence of international links, through which problems of foreign workers may be dealt with at the most senior decision-making levels of the State, in a sense bypassing the usual modes of mobilizing public opinion. The EEC regulations adopted during the 1960s, culminating in Regulation 1612 published in 1968, developed a system of free movement of national workers within the EEC (cf. Rist, 1980) and created a class of "community workers" without, however, fully envisaging the problems that would arise from the difficulties of integration. The implicit obligation on the EEC is to find suitable solutions for the educational problems of this group. In addition, countries such as France had already existing bilateral agreements regarding education with countries which had previously been colonies or protectorates. Out of this situation has grown up a complex set of multilateral and bilateral arrangements that are providing some assistance for resident foreign workers. This method of international arrangements has also been actively pursued by countries that are not members of the EEC, as may be noted from the mapping studies of Portugal, a "sending" country, and Sweden, a "receiving" country. Measures taken in response to such international agreements have the advantage, in terms of public opinion, that they are not part of an educational policy process but can be presented as part of the general fabric of policy aimed at developing national economic life. (The concomitant disadvantages of this approach, dealing with nationalities on an individual, piecemeal basis, are evident from the case studies.)

General transnational trends in support of minorities.   Perhaps the most potent factor evident from the studies as a whole, is the development of an international climate of opinion that favours more open, tolerant responses to minorities, a movement most visible from the 1970s onwards. Only one of the case studies comments on possible causes for such broad movements of opinion; the Canadian study links the changes in treatment of Francophones to phenomena such as increasing prosperity and urbanization during the post-war period that led to a gradual breaking down of some of the traditional structures of social life and opened the way for innovative approaches to minority needs.

The ambiguities of minority opinion

Policy making on education for linguistic and cultural minorities is bedevilled by the general confusion that often reigns among the minorities about the objectives that should be assigned to education. First, multiple minorities may be present, in a given jurisdiction, and different groups may have contradictory aims. Secondly, within a given minority group, there may be internal differences as between different sub-groups. Thirdly, there is often a generation gap between the children attending school and their parents; children of foreign workers, for example, may lose their attachment to the home country of their parents, seeking primarily to make a place for themselves in the new society, whereas their parents may seek to have them educated in a way permitting their eventual return to the home country. Finally, the conditions under which minority groups live may discourage the development of coherent leadership and community organizations, so that authorities do not have a unified, recognized group with which to deal in arriving at decisions about education.

The range of problems posed in dealing with minority group objectives varies rather considerably between the three main groups of minorities: established minorities, recent arrivals (immigrants or foreign workers), and indigenous people. The traditional, established minorities appear, by and large, to be the easiest to deal with, simply because they have an established place in the power structure and political life of their respective countries. In different areas of Wales, for example, decisions about use of the Welsh language are generally resolved at the level of the local school; even though opinions may differ between parents, there are well understood mechanisms for receiving, filtering and deciding on the opinions. By contrast, the description given in the three case studies dealing with recent arrivals (England, Germany, France) shows an enormous diversity of national origins, a relatively low level of community organization (except for Commonwealth immigrants to the United Kingdom), and weak, barely formalized mechanisms for obtaining opinion. The place of the indigenous peoples is somewhat ambiguous. Most have been in place for many generations and have a recognized place in their respective societies with interlocutors recognized by their educational authorities. The somewhat fragmentary indications from the reaction papers combined with the data in the mapping studies, suggests a situation where the established mechanisms are being challenged within the indigenous communities, though the pattern is fragmentary and often inconsistent. Furthermore, if one takes the example of Aboriginal peoples living in Australian urban areas, they may be present in such small numbers or so submerged by the cultural norms of a different society, that community mechanisms virtually do not exist, rendering dialogue extremely difficult except at the individual level.

The case studies outline the basic dimensions of the internal contradictions within the minority groups. The French study refers to aspirations to "collective advancement" and "individual freedom" (Limage, p. 14). The study for England and Wales summarizes the issue in one sentence: "At its simplest we can say that aspirations are either assimilationist or preservationist or combinations of the two" (Rosen, p. 21). These same issues of individual choice regarding education appear also in the discussion of Francophones in Canada, as well as in the issues raised regarding indigenous peoples. The minority group member inevitably is faced with making tradeoffs to determine what is the best way to "get ahead" educationally — by seeking to merge with the majority group or by retaining a separate identity, by trying to adapt to life in a new country or to return to a distant "home" country. This dichotomy is often deeply felt by the individuals concerned. Policy makers are faced with the problem that the dichotomy is not usually clear. Only a relatively few minority group members do succeed in integration with a new society, even over a period of two or three generations. For most minority groups studied, the issue is probably not so much whether to be different, but how much difference is necessary and useful and what differences should be, so to speak, cultivated.

The conclusions of the Canadian case study present a schema for tracing the evolution of policy concerns of linguistic and cultural minorities in terms of their reaction to the different levels of educational opportunities offered them. The stages appear to be applicable to most countries, even though it must be recognized that the internal inconsistencies of opinion within minority groups mean that the characterization will not apply to all members of a group at any time. The scheme may be summarized as follows (Churchill, pp. 51–3):

(i) *At Level 1, the recognition phase*, the minority group seeks to obtain recognition of its special educational needs and, in many cases, of its own existence as a group having a place in society.

(ii) *At Level 2, the start up and extension phase*, having obtained a limited response from educational authorities, the minority seeks to obtain the creation and extension of minority language educational services or, where these exist without sanction, the legitimation and improvement of services. The emphasis in this phase is on *quantitative* gains, in amount of instruction offered and in numbers of students served. Two types of objectives may be pursued in this phase: "Transitional" objectives concern use of the minority language and culture as a means of transition to education in the majority language, i.e. forms such as initial instruction in elementary school through the minority language, transitional "bilingual" classes, and so forth. "Group maintenance" objectives attempt to obtain policies that, to the maximum extent possible, involve use of the minority language as a means of instruction to resist assimilation pressures outside the school environment.

(iii) *At Level 3, the consolidation and adaptation phase*, where educational policies have provided access to educational opportunities for most members of the group (fulfilling the immediate quantitative need for provision), the objective becomes to improve the quality and relevance of the education received. Relevance in terms of "transitional" situations may mean emphasis on goals facilitating social and economic integration (including development of understanding of the minority culture among members of the majority), whereas in "group maintenance" situations it may mean giving recognition not only to the minority language as a medium of instruction but also to the specific culture as a source of content of instruction.

To the above may be added one more level:

(iv) *At Level 4, the multilingual co-existence phase*, educational rights for a minority cease to be a major issue. Rights are legally and practically entrenched and different language groups co-exist, not necessarily without friction, but on a basis of quasi-equality. This corresponds mainly to the situation of some of the old, established multilingual countries like Belgium and Switzerland.

The classification of different minority situations according to this scheme is highly subjective, particularly when done at a global level: different minorities in the same jurisdiction may have quite different places on the scale, dependent upon their length of residence and other factors. Table 4 shows a rough classification of minorities for a limited selection of countries. The difficulties of classification are obvious: the great majority of United States Hispanics, for example, do not have access to bilingual services, even if certain states and cities have exemplary programmes; thus, the majority might be at Level 1, but a minority at Level 2. Because of the long-standing development of social services in the Scandinavian north, the Lapps/Samit are probably to be classed in Level 2, whereas the bulk of indigenous peoples in other countries are at Level 1. Foreign workers in Western European countries pose similar problems: the breadth of coverage, in terms of proportion of workers reached, places foreign workers in Sweden and Denmark probably at Level 2, but those in France and Germany at Level 1, even if the form of the programmes

TABLE 4 *Impressionistic classification of multilingual situations for a selection of minority groups mentioned in the studies according to level of development of minority aspirations*

Level	Transition	Group Maintenace
1	Most indigenous peoples U.K. "immigrants" Resident foreign workers (France, Germany) Most U.S. Hispanics	
2	U.S. Hispanics, some states Res. foreign workers – Sweden, Denmark Manitoba (early 70s)	Lapps/Samit Finns in Sweden Catalans Ontario & Manitoba French Welsh (Level 1?)
3	?	New Brunswick French Romansch
4	Belgium, Finland, Switzerland	

Levels: 1. Recognition phase.
2. Start up and/or extension phase (quantitative development).
3. Consolidation and adaptation phase (qualitative development).
4. Multilingual coexistence phase.

offered is in some cases the same. Recent constitutional changes in Spain have shifted the Catalans, from a Level 1 to a Level 2 status, from which it is expected they would emerge to Level 3 in a short time. Because of their very small numbers, the Romansch speakers of Switzerland would probably best fit situation 3, whereas the remainder of the country's official language groups are in a Level 4 situation. The absence of any candidates for the table cell "Level 3-transition" together with the tendency of groups, such as the Francophones in Manitoba, to move from "Level 2-transition" to "Level 2 maintenance" suggests that there is little likelihood of development beyond Level 2 if the group goals are transition and integration. After a certain period, if the group goals remain transitional, the success of its members in entering the mainstream of the majority society may cause it to disappear; conversely, if it does not disappear, the longevity of the group's existence inevitably shifts it into a position of seeking group maintenance.

Even if classification of whole jurisdictions within the framework is somewhat loose, the examination of individual minority group situations in the case studies indicates that most, if not all, can easily be fitted into the schema. Its main utility is to provide a dimensioning of minority aspirations across countries, so that one can see what differences of minority aspirations confront policy makers.

Dimensions of problem definition and policy response

The regularity we have observed in the type of aspirations formulated by minority groups in response to the different stages of development of educational opportunities, suggests that there is likely to be some consistent pattern in the type of responses their aspirations generate in policy makers. This is borne out by the comparative examination of the different countries represented directly or indirectly (e.g. through response papers on indigenous minorities) in the study. In order to discern the similarities, one must distinguish between two very different situations: (i) the situation where the "usual" policy making apparatus is used in a country to arrive at solutions making use of the existing educational system, adapting it to meet the needs of minorities, and (ii) the cases where an "external" policy initiative or imperative comes from outside the normal educational policy-making environment. The latter case is represented by the recent tendency in Western Europe to arrive at agreements on treatment of resident foreign workers on a multilateral basis, as well as by cases in the United States where judicial action has resulted in the imposition of new obligations on the educational system without passing through the usual policy-making routes. The external impetus requires changes in the otherwise normal functioning of the educational system, often resulting in what might be termed "parallel" responses that are not fully assimilated into, or consistent with, the main flow of educational policy.

If one considers only the first case, where the assumption is made that the existing educational system is the main means of accommodating the needs and aspirations of minorities, the policy responses to groups having different languages (or dialects) from the majority can be grouped into a few major categories. These categories are relatively coherent wholes defined in terms of the following elements: (i) the problem definition, that is the assumptions made about the origin of the educational problem to be solved; (ii) the expected relationship between the mother tongue (first language or L1) of the minority student and the majority language (second language or L2, from the student's viewpoint) in the medium or long term; and (iii) the general type of educational provision necessary to deal with the assumed causes as defined.

The major groupings or models of problem definitions and policy responses are summarized in Table 5. If one excludes the countries with relatively old, established minority situations whose major contours were defined at least fifty, or more, years ago (Belgium, Finland, Switzerland), the models also represent what appear often to be sequential historical stages. Although no "new" or non-established minority appears to have progressed beyond the Stage 4 Model, some established minorities, such as the Franco-Manitobans, have moved from Stage 1 or 2 to Stage 5.

The lowest stage (not shown) consists simply of ignoring the existence of special educational problems of minorities or of deliberately attempting to cause their disappearance or to enforce their separateness as a subordinate class (cf. *apartheid*). Most national educational systems have gone through this stage at some point in the past. The history of literacy policy in the case studies, particularly with respect to dialects very divergent from the majority standard language, illustrates this tendency well. The development of special education in most of the systems under examination has eliminated most situations where severe disadvantage goes unrecognized at the level of the individual student, even if treatment methods may be misadapted.

Since all of the countries in the study have specific policies for dealing with at least a portion of their minorities, all have at least some policies operating at the level of the Stage 1 or 2 models. The initial recognition of the problem in most cases has defined the problem in terms of the *learning deficit model of Stage 1*, with educational provision characteristic of traditional approaches to special education. By various measures, certain groups of students are observed to suffer from scholastic deficiencies: they have poor grades, progress through the system more slowly than others, may have special discipline problems, and drop out of school in greater numbers and at earlier ages than the national norms. The *Stage 2 model of socially-linked learning deficit*, sometimes but not always arrived at concurrently with Stage 1, is recognition of the broader social problems associated with deficient school performance: the students' poor performance in school may derive from the unfavourable socio-economic situation of their parents and may lead them to fall into the same situation, characterized by a lower likelihood of making a smooth transition to the adult work world and greater proneness to serious social problems in later life, linked to low socio-economic status and poor educational attainment.

These two stages appear to be universal to OECD countries with the possible exception of two: Finland, where the Swedish-speaking minority was originally perceived by the majority as having a position of higher prestige and social attainment, and Switzerland, where the relationship between the language groups in modern times was coloured by the fact that each of the three major languages (French, German, Italian) was spoken in nearby, culturally prestigious countries, a factor tending to attenuate the superior/inferior status relationships often found in multilingual settings. By contrast, it is evident from the Canadian case study that the same initial (learning deficit) conceptualization was applied to minority Francophones, whose scholastic achievement was below that of their English-speaking counterparts.

The Stage 1 problem definition, expressed in terms of a deficit model of special education corresponds to the adoption of pedagogic measures aimed at narrowing the achievement gap. Where minority students are enrolled in the majority-language system (true of most countries except those with long-established minorities) the problem has historically been seen as a language deficit, i.e. the students have an inadequate grasp of the majority language. The French and German case studies detail a variety of special measures aimed at upgrading knowledge of the second language; educational authorities in England also appear to stress development of English skills for immigrant students. The intent is primarily to bring the students' knowledge of the classroom language up to a level where they can benefit from instruction; this is accompanied by measures of cultural familiarization in some cases, as indicated in the Danish regulations: "The purpose of Danish language teaching is for pupils to acquire proficiency in the Danish language, and to familiarise them with conditions prevailing in Denmark" (Hjorth, p. 64). The United States Title VII legislation for bilingual/bicultural education makes language deficiency the criterion of admission to such programmes (Leibowitz, 1980; 17). The United States programmes also include measures that illustrate the type of action that is characteristic of the Stage 2 model, such as programmes to facilitate job training and placement on the labour market for members of minorities. The Swedish mapping study reports the largest range of such measures, including summer programmes for immigrants and short vocational prog- rammes for all interested youths.

Even though at this stage the primary problem identified is the students' lack of knowledge of the second (majority) language, several countries have introduced instruction in the children's mother tongue for reasons not

TABLE 5   *Major models of problem definition and policy responses*

Model	Assumptions about Problem Causes	Typical Policy Responses	Language Outlook
STAGE 1: Learning deficit	Learning deficit in majority language (L2) due to use of mother tongue (L1). Problem similar to retardation or learning handicap common in special education	Supplementary teaching of L2 Special grouping for initial instruction, rapid transition to instruction in L2	L1 expected to be replaced by L2, rapid transition to L2 for school
STAGE 2: Socially-linked learning deficit	Language deficit as in Stage 1, instruction problem definition same. Causes linked to family status: broad range of problems anticipated, linked to social status, both at school and after school leaving	Teaching programmes similar to Stage 1 model. Special measures to assist adjustment to majority society: "orientation" for immigrants, vocational counselling, youth programmes, etc.	Same as Stage 1
STAGE 3: Learning deficit from cultural/social differences	Language deficit recognized as for Stages 1 and 2. Instructional problem definition same, except greater weight given to affective consequences of culture differences (e.g. concern for students' self-concept). Partial responsibility placed on society, schools for not accepting, responding to, minority culture.	Language component of teaching same as Stages 1 and 2. "Multicultural" teaching programmes: teaching about minority culture for all students, sensitization programmes for teachers, programmes of community contact. Revision of textbooks to eliminate racial, ethnic slurs and stereotyping	Same as Stages 1 and 2 for education and long-term; short-term in-family use of L1 expected, i.e. for one or two generations

STAGE 4: Learning deficit from mother tongue deprivation	Language deficit as for Stages 1, 2 and 3 but a major causal factor is assumed to be (premature) loss of L1 inhibiting learning of L2 for cognitive and affective reasons. Social problems recognized as for Stage 2. Cultural differences recognized as for Stage 3 but usually less emphasis placed on need for cultural acceptance by majority, school programmes	Language component same for L2 teaching as in Stages 1 to 3. Support provided for home language by study of L1 as a subject, sometimes also as a medium of instruction. Sometimes may include "multicultural" component for majority as in Stage 3	Same as Stage 3, except transition to L2 in school expected to take longer in most cases
VARIANT: STAGES 1–4(B) Migratory alienation	Problem definition superimposed on the definition in Stages 1, 2, 3 or 4 regarding problems of contact with, or integration into, majority schools and culture. Children are assumed to lose contact with culture of origin as result of foreign residence and require help to prepare for return to culture of origin	Teaching of majority culture language same as for corresponding stage (1–4 above). Additional instruction in L1 as a subject, often with country's geography and history taught through L1 as medium of instruction. Additional instruction often outside regular school day	Dependent upon residence: return to home language or, if remaining in new country, same as for appropriate stage of country policy (1–4 above)
STAGE 5: Private use language maintenance	Minority language of group threatened by disappearance if not supported, due to smaller numbers of minority. Minority disadvantaged in education by weaker social position of language and culture, due to smaller numbers. Minority has long-term rights to survival. Minority expected to enter majority society outside school	Minority language used as medium of instruction, usually exclusively in earlier years. Majority language required subject of study, at least from late elementary years (10–12 year-old) onward. Transition to majority language usually required for higher levels of educational system	L1 maintained as domestic, private language of group. Outside home, minority uses L2 in work, trade, business life. Long-term group assimilation if demography unfavourable

cont.

TABLE 5 cont. *Major models of problem definition and policy responses*

Model	Assumptions about Problem Causes	Typical Policy Responses	Language Outlook
STAGE 6: Language equality	Languages of minority and majority assumed to have equal rights in society. Language of smaller group may require special support to ensure broad social use: education viewed as only one field of language policy application	Minority language granted status of official language. Separate educational institutions by language, usually under administration by relevant language group. Support measures extend beyond educational system to all phases of official business, sometimes private sector as well	Indefinite, prolonged use of L1 by minority in home and in considerable part of work, business life. Long-term co-existence of minority, majority groups

Note: In the table L1 refers to the first language (mother tongue) of the minority; L2 refers to a second language, the majority language, that the minority learns/acquires.

directly related to the assumptions of the model. The most common case, illustrated by France and Germany, involves the use of language teachers from the home countries of the students (or of their parents) to teach the language as a subject and, at least in Bavaria, to use it as a medium of instruction for other school subjects; this reflects the "external" impetus referred to earlier, the objective being to facilitate eventual return. The case study for England and Wales cites a report from research in the early 1970s, in which "the authors discovered that although no official policy had been declared, the first limited steps were being taken to provide tuition" in the mother tongue (Rosen, p. 36).

Until relatively recently many educators felt that continued use of the mother tongue by students might interfere with the acquisition of the second language. Paradoxically, the contradiction between the first and second language support measures may not exist, according to mounting research evidence (Boos-Nunning, p. 50). We shall return to this point below. Meanwhile, the common sense belief in the contradiction between the support of the mother tongue and the assumption of the Stage 1 and 2 models has more influence on public opinion than do research findings.

The *Stage 3 problem conceptualization* has become rapidly more popular under the name of "multicultural education" or "multiculturalism". It assumes that minorities suffer from learning deficits at least in part because of the failure of the majority society — particularly its educational system — to recognize, accept and view positively the culture of the minority. In other words, a portion of the blame is shifted to the educational system, and, in neutral terms, one may refer to a "mismatch" between the programmes and institutions, on the one hand, and the minority needs, on the other. It is interesting that the recognition of the culture of children may be endorsed officially without provoking, however, the acceptance of the premise that the language of that culture requires support. Thus, in England the Community Relations Commission carried out, between 1968 and 1976, various programmes to support multiculturalism; however, as the case study notes, the Commission showed "little or no concern for the maintenance of the mother tongues of ethnic minorities, and the West Indian dialects are seen only as causing difficulty in learning, a viewpoint which has been challenged by many sociolinguistic scholars" (Rosen, p. 41). The essence of the model is the recognition of a right to be different and be respected for it, not necessarily to use a different language. The multiculturalism concept appears to be gaining ground in a number of Western European countries, usually with at least limited recognition of the utility of mother tongue instruction (Porcher, 1981).

The *Stage 4 problem definition* assumes that a major cause of learning deficits among linguistic minorities may be traced to linguistic deprivation, i.e. failure to develop the mother tongue of children. As mentioned above, research evidence appears to be lending support to this thesis, which is integral to educational programme definitions in a number of countries. The United Stages legislation, for example, defines bilingual education as a programme designed for children with limited English language skills in which there is "instruction ... in English and, to the extent necessary to allow a child to achieve competence in the English language, the native language of the children of limited English proficiency ..." (Para. 703(a)(4)(B), Bilingual Education Act, cited by Leibowitz, 1980: 27). Countries such as Sweden have adopted far-reaching programmes of home language support, where the goal of transition to the majority tongue is complemented, in terms of the policy statements, by more long-term objectives. A Bill passed by the Riksdag in 1975 set down guidelines for immigrants and minority group policy, with the triple aims of equality, freedom of choice, and partnership. The freedom of choice aim means that the "members of linguistic minorities must be able to choose the extent to which they will assume a Swedish cultural identity and the extent to which they will retain their cultural and linguistic identity" (Wennas, p. 28). Such an objective implies possibilities of long-term language maintenance, thus exceeding the minimum requirements, so to speak, for Stage 4. The Stage 4 model is still based largely on the concept of linguistic deficit but is enlarged to accept the need for support of the minority language at least as a transitional measure.

An examination of policies in countries having established minorities permits the identification of at least two additional stages. *Stage 5* reflects the type of thinking explicitly written into the Swedish legislation just discussed. It recognizes minority groups as being permanently weaker members of society, because of smaller numbers, but recognizes their right to maintain and develop their own languages as cultures in private life. This means that the minority languages are expected to be maintained for use mainly in the family, religion, and private social activities. Support for this role comes mainly from the use of the minority language as a medium of instruction in the educational system, particularly in the initial years of instruction. Most minority language students are expected to pursue studies in the majority language, if they go on to higher levels of education beyond some point (variable by jurisdiction). The case studies of Manitoba, New Brunswick and Ontario illustrate situations where, over the years, the age of transition to studying through the medium of the majority language has been gradually shifted upwards. The most rudimentary form of this involves initial literacy instruction in the first years of elementary school using the mother tongue, sometimes combined immediately with use of, and instruction in, the majority language. Such programmes are found today in education for indigenous peoples such as the Lapps/Samit and Maori; it is also the case of the Danish minority in Sleswig-Holstein (albeit in private schools) or the Francophones of the Valley of Aosta, in Italy. Cases such as the latter are almost indistinguishable, in terms of teaching practices, from some identified with Stage 4; the main difference is the assumption made about the long-term role of the minority group in the country involved.

Stage 6 is the granting of full official language status to the minority language for the purposes of use in public institutions. Where numbers and social dynamism permit, the minority language may also take its place in the broader economic life of the country, a situation only reached in the very old bilingual or multilingual states (Belgium, Finland, Switzerland). The widely publicized constitutional changes in Spain are obviously intended to move towards a situation like this in areas such as Catalugna. The Canadian case study illustrates some of the potential complications and/or flexibility of moving through these last two stages in a federal system: the policy of official bilingualism adopted by the Federal Government applies only to Federal institutions and services, thereby leaving out entirely the field of education, which is under provincial control. Of the three provinces studied, all have given to the French language the status of language of instruction, but only New Brunswick has also adopted it as an official language of the province for all government business.

Table 5 illustrates the major stages or models of problem definition identified across the studies, together with the typical policy response associated with each. In order to accommodate all cases, an additional variant on models 1–4, labelled "Stages 1–4 (B)", is included: it is the result of superimposing on these models the concept of preparing the students to leave their "host" country. It implies that the school system will provide foreign students with a minimum of instruction in their native language (mainly teaching the language as a school subject) along with some cultural and other information about their parents' country of origin. As the case study on England and Wales illustrates, this model may be superimposed even in situations where there is generally little willingness on other grounds to recognize minority languages for instructional purposes. The impetus in the United Kingdom appears to have come from an official commitment to abide by the Council of Europe Directive of 25th July 1977 that member countries apply a 1976 resolution of the Council; the resolution laid down obligations to provide "more opportunities as appropriate for teaching these (migrant) children their mother tongue and culture, if possible in school and in collaboration with the country of origin" (Rosen, p. 57). It should be obvious, however, that the institution of such measures creates a situation that easily leads to the Stage 4 model, in which home language deprivation is viewed as a major source of educational problems.

The differences between the various stages of the process of problem identification are not always clear-cut. Some of the United States bilingual programmes are of sufficient scope that, even though the official motivation for creating them, as expressed in legislation, corresponds to a Stage 2 or Stage 4 outlook, they are viewed by the recipients in the context of Stage 5, i.e. as tending toward long-term maintenance of group language and culture. A fundamental shift in outlook regarding the minority language separates Stage 5 and 6 from all the earlier ones. Stages 1 to 4 are primarily aimed at treating a handicap. Stages 5 and 6 seek to cultivate a difference which is viewed as a positive asset for the individual and (particularly in Stage 6) for the society as a whole.

The emphasis of this discussion has been on the general dimensions of policy objectives at the broadest level and the way these relate to different levels of educational service provision. The way these objectives are translated into policies and implemented in practice is obviously shaped by the specifics of each country's situation. The following section reviews the ways in which different policy instruments are selected and implemented, and the interactions between different options available to policy makers.

4 Policy instruments and interactions

The purpose of this section is to consider how problem definitions and related policy objectives are translated into policy instrument choices and, specifically, the way different instruments interact with each other. Legal status and framework are discussed first because they provide the structure of the policy development process. A section on organizational arrangements then serves as a backdrop to general discussion of how financial and regulatory measures fit into the total approach adopted by policy makers, what may be termed the "regulatory stance". The discussion retains the broad definition of policy instrument given earlier, that is, any of the formal means adopted to define and put into practice a given set of educational objectives.

Legal status and framework

The legal status of a given policy action is, within certain limits, a matter of decision. If one took the hypothetical example of a minister of education who wished to accomplish a certain change in the education offered to a linguistic minority, he or she might have the option of presenting a new bill for adoption as law in the legislative process, issuing a "regulation" with binding force within the limits of an existing law, issuing an administrative order through subordinates, having a circular or memorandum sent to appropriate persons with recommendations for action, using the system of educational finance to create incentives or disincentives for action, or selecting a variety of other mechanisms dictated by the circumstances. The choice exercised regarding the legal status of the policy instrument is likely to have a significant impact on the way the objectives are carried out.

The example given illustrates the more narrow case of choice in terms of the legal status of a given policy instrument, as viewed by a single actor in the policy process. Viewed across the entire range of countries in the study, the range of choice is greater. Decisions are made not only about specific instruments but, indeed, about the framework of the policy process within which the choices are exercised, and by whom. The discussion below considers, first, choices regarding the structure of the policy process and, secondly, the factors of importance in determining choices of instruments within the process, so defined.

The framework of the policy process

The different constitutional and administrative arrangements of the OECD countries provide a rich variety of situations that illustrate the main choices involved in structuring the policy development process. The main options are as follows:

Number of levels of decision making. The most noticeable cases of this concern constitutional arrangements in federal states, where division of authority between a central government and the next level of government or administration (state, province, *Länder*) are readily visible in the general political arrangements of the country as a whole. The second level of division, usually also easy to discern even from the mapping studies, concerns the degree of power conferred upon the geographical territory where schools are immediately situated — city, commune, county, borough or one of a host of names used in different countries. Some systems have specially elected bodies to make decisions on certain matters at this level; some are specialized, such as school boards (commissions, divisions) in North America, whereas others have broader attributions, such as the local authorities in England and Wales, responsible both for education and most other locally delivered social services. It is not uncommon to have relatively complex cross-representation between different bodies concerned with education at the local level, e.g. the Education Committees in Denmark with representation from the town council as well as school-level boards.

It is not possible to infer from the number of levels or participants, the amount of discretion accorded for effective decision-making. This is because the educational administration system itself, that is the administrative structures made up of career administrators are, themselves, major decision-making structures. Their operation requires, in most cases, an extremely expert and detailed examination in order for the nature of responsibilities at different levels to be understood. In almost all systems, however, one principle is understood: each level or group has specific assigned competencies that define the role it may play. Decisions about these competencies are a key variable to be manipulated in policy making.

Legitimate participants in decision-making. The administrative and governance structure has a specific system of selection of participants. From the point of view of minority education, a key issue is the extent to which groups not representing the majority view of the population have a right to be heard and represented in decision-making. We shall return to this point in the discussion of governance.

Specific attributions of decisions made by different levels and participants. Each decision in an educational system has an assigned legal status. At the most general level, legislation passed by an appropriate national or, in some cases, federative legislature, or parliament, is the summit of the status hierarchy (except for certain provisions of constitutional law). At the base one finds day to day administrative and pedagogical decisions made by teachers and administrators. In between these levels, each system interposes a surprisingly complex set of intermediate ranges of authority, not a handful but, literally, dozens in any given administrative system.

Legitimate clients of the system. One of the most important issues in dealing with minorities is the legal structure that defines the moment when they become "recognizable", so to speak for purposes of decision making. The case of resident foreign workers proved to be particularly difficult in many countries, partly because no level of the system was formally expected to deal with their needs in a collective way. This explains in part why the initial response to their needs tends to be to assimilate the ethnic and cultural minorities to the groups traditionally dealt with by special education, such as the handicapped and retarded.

The multitude of differences in respect to decision-making processes in education obviously cannot be analysed on the basis either of the mapping studies or the case studies. It is important, however, to keep in mind the underlying complexity of the phenomena being considered, together with the general principles underlying the structuring of decision-making processes. Against this background it is possible to situate both the general issue of how instruments are selected and the more narrow problem of the factors determining the selection of instruments of different legal status.

The choice of instrument status

The legal status of the different policy instruments used to guide the education of linguistic and cultural minorities often is as much a by-product of the existing structure of the policy framework as it is an object of specific choice. The following are the factors that appear most decisively to shape the choice of instruments.

Availability to the decision makers. This obvious constraint takes on particular meaning when power of decision making and implementation is spread across different "hierarchical" levels. In the Canadian constitutional system, the Federal government is severely limited in the means of action at its disposal for affecting educational policies: the case study describes the use of financial incentives within a negotiated framework as the prime means used for fostering bilingualism policies in the provinces. This exemplifies the case where the non-availability of other instruments, such as legislative measures, is determined by rigorous constitutional law. At the opposite extreme of the administrative hierarchy, the latitude for changes to be made at the level of the classroom or the school, for example with respect to programme content or language of instruction, is usually bound just as strictly by regulations and legislation controlled at a more senior level. The exception usually cited to this, namely the school autonomy of the United Kingdom educational system, is bound however by various informal and formal mechanisms (the Inspectorate, the examination system, etc.).

If one leaves aside the cases of rigid exclusion defined by formally prescribed roles, the criterion of availability becomes much more fluid: some measures are simply not available because they are not opportune, e.g. they fly in the face of current practice in a way unacceptable to public opinion or to most teachers. An example of this would be the adoption of a legally permissible option that violates usual administrative tradition. The study of England and Wales cites an occasion when the Welsh Joint Education Committee suggested an earmarked grant for bilingualism. "Although the Minister concerned (Mrs Shirley Williams) was sympathetic, the idea was opposed particularly by the national Association of Metropolitan Authorities and the Association of County Councils" (Rosen, p. 52). In rejecting a similar proposal for creating a special fund to which local education authorities could apply for resources to meet the special educational needs of ethnic minorities, the Department of Education and Science noted in 1974 that such a fund might "reduce the scope of local responsibility" (Cited by Little & Wiley, 1981: 12). The Canadian case study cites the example of Ontario, where earmarking of funds for Francophone educational expenditures was delayed for years because of the conflict with existing practice. This illustrates a principle: some conflicts with tradition render use of policy instruments unusable until the decision maker considers that the costs of failing to use the instruments outweigh the benefits of respecting customary practice. In other cases, where legal or similar constraints are interposed, the usual option is to seek to achieve the same ends by less direct means, e.g. by financial incentives when regulatory measures would otherwise have been the most direct option.

Possibilities for controls and sanctions. Certain policy instruments have a built-in system of controls that derive from the general legal and administrative framework of the educational system. Thus, in systems where a numerous and active inspectorate works to enforce the observation of good educational practices and the regulations prescribed by the responsible authorities, the issuance of a formal regulation of the type on which the inspectors may act, brings with it a full system of enforcement. In general, most policy instruments have their own enforcement mechanism; the choice is not between control and total absence of control but between the judiciousness of one system of control as opposed to another. This problem is well-known in the field of race relations, where authorities are obliged at any one time to choose between sanctions and educational measures to ensure compliance with principles of human rights; excessive reliance on sanctions can have an opposite effect from that intended.

The case studies contain ample evidence that the introduction of innovations favouring minorities may create conflictual situations, where teachers and educational administrators are obliged to adapt their behaviour to follow policies with which they may not agree. In such situations, despite the apparent contradiction, *absence* of sanctions may be an important objective in choosing the status of a given policy. This may also hold true between different levels of government: the Canadian system of formula-based subsidies to the provinces has very little accountability built into it, other than the requirement that, in order to qualify, provinces must report on numbers of students enrolled in minority language education programmes. Recent Canadian Federal policy — over the objections of the provincial governments — has attempted to redefine the relationship "... in terms of phasing down the Federal contribution under formula payments and increasing the proportion of funds channelled into 'special projects'; this amounts to increasing the control of the Federal Government over use of funds, as the specifics of each project must be mutually agreed. The limits of such a project are, of course, that there is no guarantee the provinces will consider the financial incentive sufficient to bother with the process of negotiation and attendant controls" (Churchill, p. 78). At the opposite extreme, the pressure brought by minority Francophones in Canada to obtain constitutional guarantees of their language rights could be interpreted, from their point of view, as having the advantage that sanction could be obtained through courts of law rather than through the political process, where they are outnumbered.

Symbolic value and visibility.   The proposals for constitutional change in Canada, just discussed, are a good example of a measure fostered by its proponents in large measure because it would have great visibility and symbolic value. The same may be said about the Swedish legislation of 1975 on immigrant and minority policy; the formal affirmation of the three principles of equality, freedom of choice, and partnership together with decisions regarding the "internationalization" of education in Sweden, have a symbolic effect that goes well beyond the specific educational measures that could be provided through the choice of policy instruments at a lower "status" level in the legal hierarchy.

Flexibility.   The need for flexibility to meet new circumstances is a constant preoccupation in the policy-making process. In general, flexibility is inversely related to the level of legal status accorded to a given policy instrument. This is commonly recognized in most systems, and each "level" of instrument used tends to have a prescribed degree of flexibility well-known to the users. One of the most common measures used to ensure such flexibility has to do with the definition of general objectives in a document having "higher" legal status (law, regulation or similar) and leaving the bulk of application to be made on an individual basis. This is particularly prevalent in the provision of financial assistance for minority groups. The description of Federal funding to Aboriginal education in Australia is illustrative: "Federal provisions occur through bulk grants to the States or as grants-in-aid to non-government bodies ... Budgets are developed on a project basis in response to individual proposals and the progress on the individual projects is monitored by the Department of Aboriginal Affairs (DAA) with advice from the Commonwealth Department of Education" (McKinnon & Bissett, p. 95).

If one considers retrospectively the factors outlined above, it is clear that the choice of instruments and their level involves reconciling, in many cases, very contradictory aims. Symbolic value may suggest that a given measure should be given status as a law or constitutional amendment, whereas the criterion of flexibility may suggest that the most expeditious approach would be at a much lower level of status.

Organizational arrangements

The discussion of organizational arrangements in different countries must be done in the context of the prevailing view of the problems posed by the education of linguistic and cultural minorities. If one refers back to the different models of problem definition outlined in the previous section, there is a clear break between Stages 1–4 and Stages 5 and 6, the latter applying mainly to established minorities, the former to those minorities that are "new". The case of Sweden constitutes an exception, in that characteristics of official policy are closely aligned with the objectives for Stage 5, even if educational practice and organization lags slightly behind at the Stage 4 level. As mentioned earlier, the Francophone minorities in Canada have been treated in the recent past according to schemas ranging from as low as Stage 2 upwards to Stage 6 in some cases. In the discussion of organizational arrangements, it will be useful to treat separately the two groupings of Stages 1–4 and 5–6 separately, using the cases of Sweden and the three Canadian provinces as evolutionary examples illustrating certain principles not readily visible from countries whose policies have remained essentially within the one of the two major groupings for a long time.

Instructional provisions

The arrangements made for providing instruction to minorities are usually developed as coherent wholes, where objectives, instructional content, and pedagogical organization are articulated at the same time. For purposes of comparison between different countries, certain issues can be separated out as crucial decision points regarding organization: grouping of students for purposes of instruction, the place of first and second languages in instruction, and instructional content and objectives.

Grouping of students for purposes of instruction
Three main principles can be seen at work in the delivery of instruction to minorities:

(i) dispersion of the minority into classes mixed with majority pupils, analogous to the "mainstreaming" of special education pupils:
(ii) concentration of the minority into separate groups; and
(iii) episodic teaching of highly dispersed small groups by itinerant teachers.

The last of these is represented mainly in the context of the teaching of indigenous peoples, such as the Aboriginal population in the Australian outstations. (Itinerant teachers are used, of course, for teaching specialized subjects in many systems; in the countries studied, teaching of the home language of linguistic minority pupils is often carried out this way. This use of teachers does not constitute, however, the principle of grouping *pupils* on a long-term basis for the bulk of their education, except for the non-ambulatory handicapped.)

An examination of practices across countries reveals no consensus regarding the most appropriate approach, insofar as indigenous peoples and new minorities are concerned. The same variety is found with respect to linguistic and ethnic minorities as for special education generally. Dispersion policies operate at two levels, corresponding to related but slightly separate goals. The general principle of mixing minority with majority pupils is pursued in large measure to ensure that the minority may benefit pedagogically and socially from the same treatment as the majority. In terms of learning the majority language, this is also assumed to favour language development through "natural" interactions. A second type of goal pursued is to ensure that "too many" minority pupils are not concentrated in one classroom or one school. The case studies point out two authorities with such policies — Bradford, in the United Kingdom, and North Rhine-Westphalia, in Germany. The goal in this case is to ensure that the so-called mainstream classes do not change character. As pointed out in one of the studies, there is potential contradiction between the two goals. Dispersion across different schools frequently involves methods such as bussing, which implies that the minority pupils are at school only for the period necessary for obligatory, formal instruction; they do not participate in extra-curricular activities, and the absence of contacts with their schoolmates outside the classroom discourages the formation of friendship links even during the school day.

The opposite approach, concentration of pupils, is pursued in numerous jurisdictions, either on a short-term or long-term basis. Bradford uses concentration on a short-term basis in special centres, where intensive second language training is given. Most jurisdictions appear to use such approaches, but on a decentralized basis (i.e. within local schools) for initial introduction to the second language for new arrivals. On a long-term basis, most jurisdictions appear to find it more convenient to integrate the minority pupils into local schools, at least for educational experiences they share with majority pupils. Some form of "withdrawal" (i.e. from the main classroom) appears to be generally practised for providing special instruction related to the individuals' culture and language. It would appear that in some states of the United States an exception occurs: bilingual teachers deal with mixed language groups in the same classroom, teaching alternatively in English and (usually) Spanish. The same is reported in rural communities in Manitoba for French and English.

Only in the case of established minorities does a clear hierarchy of values appear. Once the goal is not immediate transition to a majority culture but preservation of a minority "difference", the emphasis of policy begins to shift to separation. Wales presents a great range of degrees of assimilation of Welsh speakers, depending upon the area considered. Depending upon numbers, "bilingual" teaching is organized by school, "unit" (i.e. group within a larger school), linguistic stream, or special class; this occurs within a framework where the dominant language medium of instruction is English. The Canadian case studies show this variety of organization and grouping patterns generalized to a system where, insofar as possible, teaching is organized only in the language of the minority pupils with the majority language being taught as a subject. The three provinces have evolved since the mid-1960s toward progressively greater separation of the minority Francophones into their own institutions. At present Manitoba (with much smaller numbers of Francophones than the other provinces) has evolved the least far in this direction, with considerable numbers of linguistically mixed schools and classrooms reported at the elementary level and considerably less use of French as a medium of instruction of secondary level. Ontario has almost all elementary and the majority of secondary students not only in separate minority-language classes but in French-speaking schools. New Brunswick has entirely separated schools. Taking into account the variations in population density, Ontario policy established a specific hierarchy where, ranged from most to least desirable, one finds separate school buildings, separate wings or reserved portions of schools, and separate classes within schools.[1] New Brunswick policy goes well beyond the educational system and, like Belgium, Finland, Spain, Switzerland and Yugoslavia, the province provides more extensive bilingualism in other public institutions.

The difference in pupil grouping principles used for new and established minorities, illustrates that this aspect of organization is dependent in large measure upon the role played by the home language of the pupils in relation to the general objectives set by policy for their education.

The place of first and second languages in instruction

The main differences in the organization of teaching for linguistic and cultural minorities across the OECD countries lie in the roles accorded respectively to the teaching of the minority (first or home) language and of the majority (second) language. Each of the two (first or second language) may be taught as a subject or used as a language or medium of instruction.

The relationship between first and second language is not exactly reciprocal in teaching practice: because of varying periods of instruction and
because of the greater or lesser weight accorded to subjects other than
language, the two languages may be present in different curricula according to a bewildering variety of combinations. To facilitate comprehension,
we shall deal with each type of teaching separately.

All countries, including those with even the oldest established minorities, require that the minority acquire the majority language (or, in
Switzerland, a second and/or third national language) during their compulsory education. Second language curricula have two basic structures in
relationship to the minority language, sequential and parallel (or concurrent):

(i) *Sequential treatments* have three major forms:

    (a) *Immediate "immersion"* in the second language, i.e. with no
prior school instruction in the home language (the treatment is
"sequential" as the instruction follows use of the first language in
the home environment); this usually takes the form of short-term
intensive language tuition in small groups, often under the name of
"reception classes" or, in France and Switzerland, "induction
classes". The Danish regulations provide a good example of this
treatment and the type of goals pursued (Hjorth, pp. 64–65). (b)
*Short-term teaching of some subjects in the mother tongue along
with intensive second language instruction.* This corresponds with
the "short-term preparatory classes" of North Rhine-Westphalia.
(c) *Long-term teaching of most subjects using the mother tongue* as
medium of instruction along with limited instruction in the second
language, *followed by later transfer to an entirely second-language
teaching situation.* This is relatively uncommon, corresponding to
what would happen to students in the Bavarian model of long-term
"bilingual" classes upon transfer to the German system. The same
model is cited as having been in effect in Ontario prior to the
mid-1960s, involving transfer from French elementary education
to English secondary schools.

(ii) *Parallel or concurrent second language instruction* is provided in
three main formats: (a) *Additional or remedial language tuition*
provided to students already studying in courses taught through
the medium of the second language. Almost all countries provide
this type of tuition for minority group members after they transfer
into majority language instruction. (b) *Gradual transfer programmes* involve a mixture of the two languages for a variable period of

time, usually within the same class. The proportion of time spent in the second language increases gradually over the school year (in shorter courses) or over a period of years. This corresponds to the model of "long-term preparatory classes" in North Rhine-Westphalia and to the bilingual education usually provided in the United States, as well as to some instructional situations found in Swedish schools. It should be noted that language instruction occurs in two forms: study of the language as a subject and use of the language as a medium of instruction for an increasing portion of the time. (c) *Long-term study of the second language as a subject*. This occurs mainly in settings where there is relatively little emphasis on eventual transfer to study in the second language as a medium of instruction, e.g. in the Bavarian "bilingual" classes and in schooling for minority Francophones in Canada.

In a strict, structural sense, the role of the minority language in instruction might be contrasted along the same dimensions of sequential or concurrent teaching, in relation to the second or majority language. Policy decisions on educational arrangements for the minority language appear less to be oriented around structural relationships to the majority language than to the degree that the minority language can be considered an integral part of the schooling experience. The implications are both pedagogical and symbolic for the students involved. The French case study, for example, quotes a report of discussions held by Yugoslav and Italian teachers regarding the issue of whether the teaching of the home language should be integrated into the regular school programme: "The very fact that the native language is taught within the normal school curriculum *enhances its value* in everyone's eyes" (emphasis in original) (Limage, p. 42 English version). In terms of the perceived commitment of the educational system to the importance of the home language for the minority, one can distinguish in the different countries, the following, arranged from least to most commitment:

    (i) No encouragement of the home language in or outside of school.
    (ii) Official encouragement (but not necessarily commitment of resources) to teaching the home language outside school hours.
    (iii) Using the home language as a short-term transitional medium of instruction (e.g. less than two years).
    (iv) Teaching the home language as a subject in school hours (or as part of the programme for which academic credit is received).
    (v) Using the home language as a transitional medium of instruction for long periods (more than two years).

(vi) Recognizing the home language as an official or quasi-official medium of instruction for major portions of the school experience.

(vii) Creation of a separate system of education for elementary and/or secondary levels in the home language.

In this list, only the relative positions of items (ii) and (iii) appear to be debatable in terms of their symbolic value; the case studies provide insufficient information to be sure of their sequence. What is important to note is that official recognition does not efface social distinctions that originate outside the school. This, for example, applies to the Bavarian bilingual model. The German case study provides ample evidence, however, that participation in classes for minority groups of any type can have a certain stigmatizing effect both on pupils and teachers both in Bavaria and elsewhere in Germany. If popular opinion considers the minority language to be "inferior" or a mark of inferior social status (as it often is), then the positive effects of official recognition may be partially offset by this factor. This problem exists to a greater or lesser extent in all countries.

Table 6 presents a rough tabulation of different instructional modes selected from across the countries represented in the studies. Some of the data on which it is based may not be complete, but the classification provides an initial, intuitive sense of the degree of recognition given to different minority languages and dialects. It does *not* constitute a measure of the degree of social acceptance of the minorities in society at large: the multicultural efforts made in many of the English educational authorities, for instance, are not shown here, but their effect in terms of breaking down out-of-school social barriers may be greater than some higher level of linguistic recognition found in other countries' official policies. A column has been added at the end of Table 6 to distinguish between three main forms of instruction given in the majority (second) language in parallel with whatever is the general form of educational provision: (a) short-term, intensive transitional instruction, (b) long-term remedial type additional instruction, that may be prescribed on an individual basis or given to groups, and (c) study of the second language as a regular school subject on a long-term basis when the dominant medium of instruction is the minority language.

The Table illustrates the main types of differences found in the degree of recognition of the minority language as well as the type of variety that may be found in even one country. Two countries are represented by entries both for new and for established minorities, Switzerland and the United Kingdom. In each case, a clear distinction can be seen in the form of educational provision made. To the author's knowledge, a similar distinction is made in most other relevant jurisdictions (Belgium, Canada, Finland), with the higher level of recognition being reserved always for the established minority.

In all but a few cases, the classifications shown reflect an evolution of policy that has occurred within the last ten years: the picture would have been much different had the data been collected in 1970 and would have been unrecognizable if one were to classify the situation in 1965: few jurisdictions would have had a check anywhere except in column (i). What is not certain, is whether the evolution of the past few years is likely to continue in the future, particularly at the juncture separating column (v) from column (vi). Both Bavaria and Sweden have forms of education that appear to be verging on those heretofore reserved for recognized minorities, albeit with very different premises. The Bavarian reliance on the mother tongue of the minority as a medium of instruction must be interpreted in the light of the critical remarks presented in the case study regarding the effectiveness of measures preparing the students for transition to the majority educational system and life in the majority German-speaking society. *If* the students so trained do not return to their home countries, the apparent policy dilemma will be a choice between stopping their education at a certain level or providing access to more advanced education in some hybrid form of school where the mother tongue has a role to play. In the case of Sweden, the combination between certain options at the elementary level for national classes (i.e. made up of students all of a single linguistic group) and experimental secondary school programmes for speakers of Finnish appears to be a move in the direction of recognizing Finnish within a limited context as a language of instruction, perhaps in a fashion analogous to the role of Swedish in Finland.

Special curriculum arrangements in non-linguistic areas

In most cases where the language of a new linguistic minority is taught, either in school or outside it, the teaching includes elements of the culture and history of the country of origin. The German case study notes the extensive use of textbooks in various subjects printed in the countries of origin and notes that the curricula are not those in German schools. The absence of detailed discussion of special curricular arrangements for minority children in almost all the studies being reviewed, must be considered the sign of an important potential problem to which little attention appears to have been devoted. The established minorities, by the very fact of their long existence in their respective countries, have an identifiable place in society and, even if problems of curricular content may

TABLE 6   *Role of the home language of minority pupils in selected jurisdictions and forms of instruction*

	i	ii	iii	iv	v	vi	vii	L2*
United Kingdom: West Indian dialects	x							2
Australia: Aboriginals	x		x (ex-perim.)					2
Denmark		x						1, 2
Switzerland (immigrants)		x						1, 2(?)
United Kingdom: non-English speaking immigrants		x						1, 2
France		x		x (elem.)				1, 2
Berlin, North Rhine-Westphalia: preparatory classes		x	x					1, 2
United States: (Bil. Ed. Act)			x	x	x			1(?),2
North Rhine-Westphalia: long-term preparatory classes				x	x			2, 3(?)

arise, they are hardly of the same type that confronts the educators serving new minorities whose long-term social role may not be adequately reflected in programmes designed for the majority. The Swedish mapping study does indicate, however, one innovative programme of a type not mentioned elsewhere: two types of special courses given during summer to young immigrants, the purpose being to attract them into further study at the upper secondary level, that is into the more prestigious levels of education giving eventual access to specialized higher training. Although not specifically mentioned as the primary target clientele, young immigrants are apparently also eligible for, and participate in, three or four other

	i	ii	iii	iv	v	vi	vii	L2*
Bavaria: 'bilingual' classes				x	x	?		2, 3
Sweden: options				x	x	x**		1, 2
United Kingdom: Wales				x	x	?		3
Manitoba: secondary				·	x	?		3
Manitoba: elementary					x	x		3
Ontario						x		3
Switzerland: Romansch				x (sec.)		x (elem.)	x	3
New Brunswick						x	x	3

Note: Table based on data in case studies and mapping studies. Classification does not include all experimental forms or variants and is subject to error. Classes i–vii described in text.

*   Second language (majority language) teaching forms:
(1) short-term, intensive transitional instruction;
(2) long-term remedial-type additional instruction;
(3) study as a subject on a long-term basis.

**   Classification vi refers for Sweden only to experimental groups in Finnish leading to secondary school graduation.

specialized programmes intended for unemployed youth (short vocational training courses, guidance courses for choice of further study and selection of career, and experimental vocational training introductory courses for drop-outs and the poorly motivated).

In the absence of specific information, it appears that most countries have not made major revisions to curriculum content other than language content, in order to meet the special needs of new linguistic and cultural minorities, particularly with reference to their entry into the majority society and the work force.

The administrative framework

The administrative framework employed for the education of linguistic and cultural minorities is, in most cases, an integral part of the framework used for the whole educational system of each country or jurisdiction studied. Rather than recapitulate the details of general school system organization found in the sub-studies for this project, the discussion that follows will focus on a limited number of issues that are specific to the problem at hand: the relationship between different levels of administration in minority education, the criteria for establishing separated teaching units for minorities, and the supervision of teachers. A fourth component of the administrative system, namely the framework for managing financial affairs, is best discussed in connection with financial instruments in the next section.

Levels of administration and minority education

Because different educational systems are characterized by radically different measures of centralization and decentralization of administration, it is common to raise the generic question as to which is a better means of meeting the needs of minorities. This may be missing the point entirely, for two reasons: First, most discussions of centralization/decentralization concentrate on overt, visible structures; when the much less visible elements of actual decision-making process and exercise of power are incorporated, most modern educational systems appear as extremely complex entities, very hard to classify on a single dimension of degree of centralization. Secondly, since most educational administrative arrangements are set up to cope with a variety of constraints, of which minority group education is only one, the likelihood that the findings of a study such as this would have an effect on policy making, would be extremely low. The main issues to be considered are not centralization or decentralization but these:

(i) How does the presence of different levels of administration and the interaction between levels affect minority education?

(ii) To what extent does the integration or separation of administration of minority educational programmes have an effect on their development and delivery?

The available case material does not permit a complete or final answer to these questions, but certain tendencies are discernible.

Recognition of minority needs appears to occur according to different processes, depending upon the level of administration concerned. At the local (i.e. school or municipal/communal/county) level, problem recognition derives largely from classroom-related problems, either as reflected by teachers' problems or parental concerns (often those expressed by the majority parents about deteriorating conditions for their children). At more central levels, classroom-level pedagogical issues are obviously considered, but there is a tendency to react in response to broader concerns as well. The Canadian Federal Government's initiatives in bilingualism derive from concerns about the future of the structure of the Canadian confederation; national governments in Western Europe have entered into agreements related to minority-language education in part through the process of developing international economic links. These issues are linked closely to methods of governance and political representation and will be discussed at length in a later section.

Implementation of policy responses involves different trade-offs depending upon the number of administrative levels concerned. The case studies comment at length on the difficulties of central co-ordination and execution of policy in systems with multiple levels of decentralization, e.g. in Canada, Germany and the United Kingdom. On the other hand, in looking across the entire spectrum of countries, it is clear that the centralized ones (i.e. in the sense of overt structural centralization and major central policy-making) face different problems. The most serious is that their operational modes do not encourage experimentation with different forms of educational provision in different parts of the same jurisdiction, so that the variety of responses found in countries such as the United States or Germany are often lacking. Thus, whereas uniform policy responses are more "simple" to execute in centralized systems, the likelihood of major innovative responses may be decreased because of the tendency to proceed in a uniform manner for most of a jurisdiction. The trade-offs are not uniform, as can be seen from a glance at the distribution in Table 6, where both centralized and decentralized systems are intermingled in their policy responses.

Setting up separate, specialized administrative structures for minorities tends to be limited to the minimum considered absolutely necessary for functioning until the policy objectives of a system reach a level corresponding to a Stage 5 problem definition (Table 5), corresponding approximately to level v or vi of recognition of the minority language. This applies both to "central" ministry and local or school level administration. A significant exception to this rule is found in the case study of England and Wales: Bradford operates 12 immigrant education centres and Coventry has set up a Minority Group Support Service. Whether this exception is of the type that tends to prove a rule or is simply an artifact of the absence of local data in other studies, is difficult to say. It does reflect a uniquely British problem, namely the administration of "targeted" programmes where a major portion of decision making is decentralized to the level of individual schools; the absence of organizational structures at a level above the school makes targeted programmes difficult to co-ordinate and control — as indicated by the case of Coventry, where one group of teachers recruited for the special programme (Section 11 programme) were attached to schools directly and subsequently proved somewhat difficult to link with the central support service.

Within jurisdictions pursuing objectives at the Stages 5 and 6 level, there is a tendency to develop separated administrative functions for minority language education. This can occur at very different levels. In Wales and Graubünden Canton, the devolution of responsibility for education is part

TABLE 7   *Linguistic separation of administrative structures for selected established minorities*

	Regional Autonomy	Minister/ Secretary	Deputy Minister	Ministry Staff	Local Authority	School
Switzerland (Graubünden)	I	N/A	N/A	N/A	N/A	S (elem.) I (sec.)
Wales	I	I	N/A	I	I	S (elem.) I (sec.)
Manitoba	I	I	I	S	I	S (elem.) I (sec.)
Ontario	I*	I	I	I	I	S
New Brunswick	I*	I	S	S	S	S

*	None of the Canadian provinces have policies of regional autonomy for linguistically defined areas, though in many areas the local administration may be dominated by the minority owing to local demography.
I	Integrated linguistically (i.e. majority language as dominant language)
S	Separated linguistically
N/A	Not applicable or information not available

of a larger transfer of powers; the Secretary of State for Wales and the Canton government have responsibility for numerous other aspects of local administration. In New Brunswick, the separation of the French and English administrations begins at the level of Deputy Minister, with parallel ministerial structures for programme-related matters and linguistically separate local school authorities operating schools in their respective languages.[2] Manitoba and Ontario have maintained linguistically integrated local school authorities. They differ in that: (a) Manitoba has a lesser degree of linguistically separated schools (owing to sparse population in rural areas) than Ontario. (b) Conversely, Ontario has a dispersed central ministerial administration, whereas in Manitoba most central functions for French education are concentrated in a single service, reporting to an Assistant Deputy Minister.

It is interesting to note that the cases of large scale devolution of powers in spheres other than education (Wales and Graubünden) are not accompanied by a high degree of separation in administration; the devolution principle is regional rather than linguistic, even if linguistic issues played a part in each case. The different degrees of separation are illustrated in Table 7. The possibility of separation at the level of minister of education is included for completeness. This can be said to occur within multilingual federations where regional autonomy is language-based (Canada, Switzerland, Yugoslavia) and in rare cases within non-Federal structures (e.g. Belgium).

Criteria for establishing separate teaching units

A crucial decision faced in dealing with linguistic and cultural minorities is that of deciding to establish a separate teaching unit (class or other grouping, sub-unit of school, or school). Decisions on creations of schools in minority situations in Canada are cited as a cause of considerable local political conflicts. It would appear that the data from the project indicate the presence of three situations:

(i) *Minority language education is considered as a right of the individual within a specific, limited territory.* In this case, the criterion for constitution of a teaching unit is automatically conferred: an individual application suffices. This would be the case where the minority language has the status of an official language and the individual is in the appropriate territorial area (Belgium, Finland, New Brunswick, Switzerland).

(ii) *Minority language education is considered a group right within a defined territory, subject to the presence of "sufficient" numbers.*

The decision regarding sufficiency of numbers is largely a function of available resources and is generally left to administrative decision-making processes without formal guidelines. This case applies to most jurisdictions reviewed in the project. Differences occur in the degree of "pressure" placed upon the appropriate decision makers regarding the accommodation of small numbers of students within existing resources. One option used is similar to that found in legislation and regulations for other types of special education: if the authority or the school cannot provide the necessary service, it must be purchased from another, nearby educational unit (Cf. The Swedish regulations in Skolöver-styrelsen, May 1979).

(iii) *Education is considered a right, independently of numbers*, and the inability of the student to understand the majority language is not considered a basis for denying that right. This particular form of provision first arose through court action in the Lau case under-taken under the 1965 Civil Rights Act in the United States. The criteria for constitution of a teaching unit or situation appear to be a matter for decision through court enforcement orders (though subsequent United States legislation and regulations appear to be shaping the criteria). This "right" appears to be limited to certain jurisdictions and subject in each case to judicial interpretation. However, it is part of a larger change affecting all of special education: "difficult" cases that previously were excluded from publicly supported special education are now being protected by new legislation (cf. MacMillan & Meyers, 1979 and bibliography cited therein).

From the point of view of the minorities concerned, case (ii) is the most common, and it is obviously a source of concern, at least for a portion of the minorities involved, that the right is subject to criteria of numbers rather than absolute. If the educational alternative available for the minority is perceived as being stigmatizing or no more related to the minority's goals than the regular majority provision (if both forms are equally "alienating", as some minority leaders would phrase it), then the concern for the specific criteria that result in creation of specialized teaching, is low. But in cases where the provision is valued by the minority, as in the case of the Francophone minorities in Canada for example, then the absence of a clear guarantee that teaching units will be available, can then become a major political issue, leading to demands for recognition of an unequivocal individual right of the type associated with an official language.

Supervision of teachers

The case studies reveal a recurring concern that is obviously in direct relationship with the quality of education offered to linguistic and cultural minorities: supervision of teachers. More is at stake than the simple hierarchical relationship necessary for drawing a pay cheque. The issue is how the teacher fits into the larger administrative framework, the *encadrement*, to use a French term. Let us look briefly at some of the major symptoms of difficulty: the French case study deals with the isolation of foreign teachers from their colleagues, attributed in part to a situation where some of them teach outside the regular school programme or (in relation to the *tiers temps pédagogique* at elementary level, in competition with activities that children find more enjoyable (Limage, pp. 41–42). The German case study gives a distinctly negative picture of teaching conditions, even for the German teachers serving minorities. Inspection of foreign teachers is also an issue, particularly in cases where the foreign teacher may be under pressure from his/her own government not to follow the curriculum of the host country (cf. Boos-Nunning, Section III.C (i)). For quite different reasons, the Australian mapping study indicates that "high teacher turnover of white teachers in some schools means that there is continual reinvention of the wheel and little energy for forward progress" (McKinnon & Bissett, p. 97).

The picture that emerges from this and other fragmentary information is one where, unless special measures are taken, the teacher of ethnic and cultural minorities can be assigned a status of a second-class member of the teaching profession dealing with second-class members of society.

The examples and problems alluded to are drawn mainly from the studies dealing with new minorities and indigenous groups, i.e. those groups whose status in their host societies is most tenuous. If one turns to the established minorities, the contrast is obvious. The teachers are regular members of their profession with normal opportunities for advancement, at least within their own language system of education. The case study of Ontario also points out a supervisory practice: if the minority language teacher teaches in an isolated situation, e.g. in a class for French pupils located in an English school and/or school board, a special French-language supervisory officer is designated for the task, either a "senior-ranking Francophone employed by the board ... (or) a person 'borrowed' from another board or from regional offices of the Ministry of Education" (Churchill, p. 74). This refinement is apparently not considered feasible and/or necessary in the neighbouring province of Manitoba, but its existence points to a concern of teachers to be treated fairly by people who recognize and share their problems. Supervision is only one element, but an important one, in the definition of status of teachers. It represents an area where countries dealing with new minorities are obviously going to have to make serious organizational improvements.

Support and ancillary services

The final area of concern in terms of organizational arrangements is that of support and ancillary services. The case studies and mapping studies make mention of them but without providing full information. Again, the same division exists as was noted for supervisory services, between the relatively well-off established minorities and the new minorities and indigenous peoples.

Support for classroom teaching

In a modern majority-language educational system, teachers can look outside their rooms for a variety of support measures: specialist advice, reference materials on teaching topics, referral servicers for special education and remedial education problems, and so on. The obvious case for the teacher of new linguistic and cultural minorities as well as for most indigenous peoples, is that such services are largely lacking. Various studies refer to experimental development of teaching materials. None refers to one of the endemic problems of minority group teaching, the misclassification and consequent stigmatization of minority pupils through improper use and/or interpretation of psychological and other tests. United States data from the early 1970s indicated, for example, that although Spanish-speaking Americans represented 9.5% of the school-age population, they comprised 32% of those labelled mentally retarded (Semmel, Gottlieb & Robinson, 1979: 229). The absence of adequately normed tests and/or specialized personnel in this area can obviously have massive consequences for large parts of minority populations. There is little evidence that this problem is being addressed at all for most of the new minorities, as well as for many of the indigenous peoples. The Canadian case study outlines, in contrast, extensive support measures of a type similar to those available to majority pupils and their teachers, though noting: "Generally speaking services for Francophones tend to be weaker than for Anglophones, though the differences between boards are greater than between language groups in individual schools" (Churchill, p. 75).

Teacher preparation and training

The same bleak picture repeats itself with respect to teacher preparation and training, aggravated perhaps in the case of many home language teachers for new minorities. Even when they have proper training in their own countries (and many do not), the foreign teachers employed frequently for this task, will normally not have received specialized training for dealing with students of their own culture who have begun to assimilate both linguistically and culturally into a new society. The German case study indicates that some minority pupils participate unwillingly in, or are confused by, home language and culture classes that use different methods and are authoritarian. A related problem, perhaps even more severe, can occur in those situations where pupils are classified by the nationality of their parents and sent to "home language" classes taught in the official language of their home country, even though the pupils may be a linguistic minority at home, too.

The problem of teacher training has been recognized and the first encouraging steps have been taken. The French case study outlines the new "CEFISEM" system of centres for specialized training of teachers who deal with foreign children. Colloquia and other exchanges on teacher preparation have also been initiated on a multilateral basis by the Council of Europe, indicating that changes can be anticipated (Joubert, 1982).

The comparatively high standards of teacher training for established minorities need only be mentioned: the Canadian provinces studied, for example, all have French or bilingual university-based faculties of education operating in French, based on an older tradition of French-language normal schools for elementary education dating back more than a century. Two colleges of Education in Wales are designated as bilingual colleges. The case study notes the interesting point that, when recent restrictions were placed on all types of teacher training, they were applied so as to safeguard the supply of bilingual Welsh-speaking teachers.

Towards an interpretation of organizational arrangements

The disparities in organizational arrangements between new and established minorities, as well as between the latter and indigenous peoples, can be attributed in part to the stage of development reached in the relevant educational sub-systems. The stages outlined for minority aspirations in an earlier section correlate highly with the stages of organizational development sketched here. The established groups are largely in the consolidation and adaptation phase, i.e. in a phase where emphasis is on qualitative developments, such as improvement of ancillary services, curriculum materials and the like. The new minorities and indigenous peoples are usually either in the recognition phase or the start up and extension phases.

As minorities are the direct clients of the educational system, their aspirations reflect rather closely the classroom experience, the other side of the organizational coin, so as to speak. To the extent that their aspirations can be used as a guide to policy, it is highly likely that the passage of time will lead to policy evolution in response to the stages outlined for aspirations. Perhaps coincidentally, this evolution is supportive of the improvements that specialized teachers ordinarily would pursue in their own interest.

The Canadian case study outlines a theoretical construct to explain how the congruence of interest comes about. It refers to the provision of services in the language of a minority but can be generalized to the case where the cultural minority speaks the majority language: The "expected level of service" is based upon the most valued dimension of the service relevant to the minority, its language (or, for groups like indigenous peoples, the cultural component of a different world outlook). The minority client of the system expects to receive services using this valued dimension initially in the classroom, e.g. through the use of the language or culture in pupil instruction. The greater the usage of the language (or culture) the higher the level of perceived service. Secondary services are those services that support the classroom experience, either through the medium of the teacher or others (psychologists, school staff, specialized guidance personnel, social workers, etc.). Progressively higher levels of service are perceived to be received, the more the secondary services adopt the client language (or culture), insofar as the adoption has a perceptible effect on the primary service directly received by the client (in-class instruction, direct teaching, or counselling). Irrelevant services from the point of view of effect (e.g. what language is spoken by the person handling the teacher's payroll slip in a central office) are excluded from the concept of expected level of service.

At some point, one may not be able to infer the value of a secondary service from its logical connection with a primary service to pupils, but from its symbolic connection to group aspirations, e.g. the presence in senior administrative posts of persons from the same language or cultural group to provide leadership.[3] If the teacher belongs to the affected minority group (i.e. shares the same culture or language), all the improvements in service according to this schema will be directly in the personal interest of the teacher both as a minority group member and as a professional whose tasks are made easier by the provision of appropriate support and ancillary services.

Financial instruments and regulatory stances

The generic question to which this section addresses itself is this: "What is the role played by financial instruments in the provision of education for linguistic and cultural minorities?" The context of this question is provided by the earlier OECD study: *Educational Financing and Policy Goals for Primary Schools*. Provision for special education needs is raised in that study as part of the broader discussion of the role of different financial instruments in pursuit of the policy goal of equalization. The following observations may serve as a starting point for discussing the issues:

"The most common approach to providing additional resources for children with special educational needs is through the use of categorical programmes ... Under this approach, recommended or required levels of service and the availability of categorical grants are often found in tandem, jointly reinforcing each other. Rules and regulations about levels of service go hand-in-hand with financial incentives, reimbursement arrangements and the like.

"A second approach used to finance special educational needs employs a 'pupil weighting' system. Rather than providing assistance to localities through separate aid programmes, this approach uses the basic equalization formula for distributing additional monies. Pupils with special educational problems are counted extra for purposes of central government allocations.

"A new development in many of the countries has been the recognition that more money alone is unlikely to overcome the problems of special educational groups and that new approaches to the provision of education are required ... Another noteworthy change in the area of special needs has been the development of new accounting mechanisms which attempt to ensure that resources which are appropriated for target populations will actually be spent on them" (Noah & Sherman, 1979: 56–57).

The results of the current project are in essential agreement with the main lines of this analysis. In addition they throw additional light on the interrelationship between financial instruments and local control of education, discussed in the primary school study under the theme of "locus of control". The primary study distinguished between three main types of inter-governmental transfers or funding mechanisms: "block (general purpose); service-specific, non-categorical (for education, or housing, or

roads, etc.); and categorical (for teachers' salaries, school building con-
struction, or educational programmes for the disadvantaged and so
forth)". The analysis found, except for the case of Australia, "a very strong
pattern of relationship between the mode of inter-governmental grant for
education and the level of local autonomy; non-categorical modes of
funding imply higher levels of local autonomy than do categorical modes".
The reason, the authors found, was that categorical grants could quickly
turn into blank cheques, so that the inevitable result was the "imposition of
standards, controls and limits" on the resources which are reimbursed
(Noah & Sherman, 1979: 58–59).

The limitations of the discussion that follows are imposed by the nature
of the data available in the current project. Out of the four case studies,
only two (Canada, England and Wales) provide detailed discussions of
financial issues and instruments. The mapping studies, on the other hand,
provide a broad panorama but lack much of the specifics that would be
necessary for direct comparison with the case studies. However, looking at
them as a whole in conjunction with the published reports on the primary
school project, certain conclusions may be drawn.

Modes of financing

In dealing with linguistic and cultural minorities, almost all jurisdictions
for which sufficient data is available to classify, have opted for categorical
funding. Separate programmes of categorical funding are used even in
systems where the main mode of financial transfer is non-categorical, with
a few exceptions to be discussed further below. This was already the fact in
many jurisdictions at the time of the primary school project; in the United
States, for example, a state such as Florida which used non-categorical
funding as the main means of financing local education, nevertheless used a
budgetary system with tight controls to ensure that the funds were
disbursed on the specific populations whose needs were used as weighting
factors in determining subsidies to localities — thus achieving exactly the
same controls as are associated with categorical earmarked funds. Since
that study there has been a change in at least one of the jurisdictions that,
at that time, used "pupil weighting" procedures; Ontario has shifted to a
resource reimbursement scheme during the interim in order to ensure that
funds are spent on Franco-Ontarians.

One salient exception is, of course, the United Kingdom's system of
block grants to local authorities. The bulk of funds flows to the authorities
through the "rate support grants", i.e. a system of grants that provide tax

relief to local authorities for the entire range of their service needs, of which education is only one. The proportion going to education is a local, rather than national, decision. It is interesting that, even in this case, there is an exception, to the exception, so to speak: the "Section 11" grant scheme. These grants constitute a *de facto*, though not *de jure*, categorical education grant for education of Commonwealth immigrants living within the authority's boundaries. Although they are not earmarked for education, 85% of the grants are regularly spent on education. Since the grants are negotiated on the basis of application from local education authorities, they are certainly far from discretionary funds under local control (Rosen, pp. 45–46). The amounts involved are a relatively small proportion both of total education expenditure and of expenditures on education of immigrants; however, they have obviously played a major incentive role in local authorities, and their existence in spite of the usual financing system is a reflection of the same type of pressures felt elsewhere in respect of the needs of minorities.

Another partial exception is the province of New Brunswick. Most local education authorities are separate English-language or French-language entities, and the unilingual local authorities are treated equally, independently of language. The grant scheme is by nature categorical, but the categories are not related to language or culture (except for a very minor weighting factor based on language mix and applicable in principle to either language group). This exception might be considered in parallel with the situation in Switzerland: at the level of the Confederation, the separate Canton of Graubünden receives subsidies. However, these are not directly linked to Romansch educational problems but to the general status of the canton, according to the data available in the mapping study. The Canadian case study also notes, in discussing some aspects of Federal subsidies to education, that Quebec does not make language-specific redistribution of funds within its educational system. The three parallels suggest that the acquisition of a status of apparent equality (accession to cantonal status, separate and largely independent school systems) may provide the grounds for not providing language-specific subsidies.

The parallels also point to a potential problem of terminology. "Categorical" systems, as defined for the needs of the primary school project, cannot be assumed to be defined in terms of specific special education populations. The degree to which the categorical grants orient decision making by the recipients is dependent upon the precise definitions given in the financial instruments. Therefore, even if we have concluded that the great majority of jurisdictions have opted for categorical funding, it cannot be assumed that this is automatically linked to a reduction in discretionary powers. Some categorical systems leave very large room for local initiative and decision-making. In the case of linguistic and cultural minorities, nevertheless, the tendency is to use categorical schemes as a means of ensuring special treatment for the populations concerned. The exceptions in Canada and Switzerland are worthy of note precisely because they go against this tendency to focus on a given population, once the population reaches a status approaching equality.

Thus far the discussion has dealt with educational finances in the same context as most other studies, i.e. national and sub-national systems of finance. This study has brought to the fore the existence of a new mode of finance: *extra-national subsidies to minority language education*. This takes two forms. In dealing with the needs of resident foreign workers, some Western European countries have opted for a system of allowing the home country of the workers to identify teachers of the same nationality, train them, and pay them. The host country typically provides free use of classroom space and, in some cases, educational materials and other support. Most of the home-language education of foreign children in France is paid for in this way, for example. A second, related form of subsidy has arisen through the action of supranational organizations such as the European Economic Community. Since 1974, for example, the British Government has made applications to the EEC Social Fund in respect of special language teaching and other provision made for immigrant children and has used the money obtained from the fund to make retrospective reimbursements to some local authorities of their portion of expenditure under Section 11 programmes. The long-term implications of such financial systems are hard to predict, but their rapid development in the field of teaching the home language of resident foreign workers is a major innovation of the last decade and is well worth further study.

Objectives of financial instruments

If one seeks to determine why special financial arrangements are made for linguistic and cultural minorities, the problem subdivides into three components: (a) the educational objectives of the policy pursued, (b) the technical basis of subsidy, and (c) the instrumental objectives of subsidization, that is the way the subsidy relates to the administrative and political environments and results in the mobilization of resources to serve the policy objectives. In a previous section, we have dealt generally with the issue of objectives, so that our discussion will be limited to the last two points.

Technical basis of subsidy

In simple terms, one is concerned to know why a special revenue flow should be associated with the education of a linguistic or cultural minority. All the schemes for categorical subsidization are based on providing a supplement to educational authorities or institutions above the "normal" amount. In other words, each system is based on some explicit notion of an additional cost, above that which the authority or institution would ordinarily be expected to cover from its regular revenues. In jurisdictions with tightly controlled systems of regulating resource flows (e.g. by fixing norms for teacher:pupil ratios and making reimbursements of teacher salaries), the additional subsidy is an automatic by-product of making changes to regulations governing the flows (e.g. by setting different pupil:teacher ratios for classes, as in the case of France). In "looser" systems the funds may be allocated on bases that are not strictly tied to a defined type of expenditure and may involve no control over expenditures. The most obvious case of absence of control is the system of transfers from the Canadian government to the provinces on the basis of minority language pupil enrolments: the absence of control and, therefore, of a direct Federal hand in the provincial jurisdiction, is an integral part of the system. Other systems, such as those in Ontario and Manitoba, involve setting certain norms for the regular instruction of persons belonging to the majority, then reimbursing demonstrable costs incurred on behalf of the minority that exceed the norms.

The crux of these systems is, in all cases, the assumption that more intensive effort and utilization of resources is necessary to cope with the needs of a minority. In this context, the exceptions mentioned earlier with respect to categorical grants in New Brunswick, Quebec, and Switzerland can best be understood: if two linguistically separated but quasi-equal educational systems co-exist in the same jurisdiction, special grounds must be found before differential subsidization of one group can be justified.

The discussion above has dealt with the provision of subsidies to current operating costs of instruction, such as teacher salaries and teaching materials. In some situations, ancillary costs may take on particular importance. With widely scattered populations, such as some indigenous peoples, and in rural areas, transportation costs may represent a significant portion of educational provision. Policies on such matters are quite variable, and no clear trends are visible in terms of financing.

The creation of new services for minorities where none have previously existed or where the minority was not dealt with on a special basis, can give rise to subsidies for *start-up costs*. Manitoba operates a so-called "development grant" that is based on quantitative increases in the amount of instruction given in the minority language for a given group of students. Ontario provides a start-up grant for creation of new instructional units to provide for such expenses as purchase of library and teaching materials, extra recruitment costs and so forth. *Programme and curriculum development* is obviously partly included in these grants; it is more specifically provided for in the financing systems of Australia and the United States, where special project funding may be available for experimentation and development of materials. Special programmes for development of curriculum materials and publication of books are also mentioned in some cases (Ontario French Language Development Fund, translation and publication of textbooks in the five dialects of Romansch in Graubünden, etc.).

Instrumental objectives of subsidy

Because most educational systems leave different degrees of discretion in execution of policy, financial instruments must be well matched to their objectives. In this sense, even in closely regulated systems, every financial component has a definable "incentive" value. Explicit incentive schemes are usually reserved to situations where there is a degree of resistance to the policy being proposed; the more the recipients of the subsidy are interested in the scheme's objectives, the less need for incentive. In systems with shared local/central finances, the most simple method is to use the central funds to pay a part, but not all, of the costs of a given programme. This constitutes a way of making it easier to shift local priorities: the Section 11 grants in England and Wales pay 75% of costs of approved programmes; this means that the shift of one pound of expenditure from another potential priority into the Section 11 programme results in an immediate "multiplication" effect, equivalent to an extra three pounds. The system used in Ontario to reimburse local authorities 100% for additional costs of Francophone education (within certain limits and guidelines) is a higher level of incentive compared to the British example, but it represents a reduction in the incentive level previously existing: some boards were spending more on English than French while receiving the special French subsidy, thereby providing, so to speak, a profit margin for the majority (and, often, a reduction in local tax levels). The case study links this shift not to a desire to reduce incentives for accomplishing a given policy goal but to a shift in policy priorities: the previous system had the effect of favouring quantitative expansion of the number of pupils served, whereas the new one tends to shift more funds into differential provision of services.

Methods of subsidization often include standard provisions that have a very different effect depending upon the jurisdiction or institutions affected. Thus, if a service for a special group already exists in certain jurisdictions but not in others, a decision at a higher level to subsidize the specific services across all jurisdictions, provides additional revenues without additional expenditures in the places where the service exists. The Canadian system of Federal subsidies for minority language education had this effect for Quebec, which had the most developed system in the country for its (English-speaking) minority, long before the other provinces began making serious efforts to develop similar provisions for the French-speakers in their jurisdictions. Since the largest share of the transfer payments for bilingualism has always gone to Quebec, it must be assumed that this artifact of the system was an integral part of its conception and may have reduced traditional Quebec opposition sufficiently to permit the first major Federal initiative related to the field of elementary and secondary education.

Some systems have rules against supplanting one funding source by another for existing programmes (cf. bilingual programme provisions in various states of the United States), but funding authorities may be loathe to use them, both because of technical difficulties and because they penalize jurisdictions that have shown initiative in dealing with a given problem while favouring those that have failed to do so.

The discussion of technical rationales for subsidy has distinguished between jurisdictions where subsidy follows higher level regulation almost automatically, and those where autonomous decisions to follow a policy orientation are required before an additional revenue flow starts. Both systems are technically based upon assumptions about additional investment of resources to meet differential needs. The implications in instrumental terms of a subsidization method depends upon the specific way the resource flows affect the actors in any given situation. Here it should be pointed out that the underlying principle of incentive schemes applies even in supposedly very centralized systems. Failure to judge carefully the implicit incentive effects of financial instruments can result in serious obstacles being placed in the way of policy implementation.

Regulatory effects of financial instruments

In Chapter 2, three types of policy instrument are distinguished: organizational changes, regulatory measures, and financial measures. These distinctions are somewhat arbitrary, as any practicing policy-maker knows. In highly centralized systems, as has been pointed out, the issuance of regulations governing educational provision often implies an automatic financial or resource flow component. Even in highly decentralized systems, financial measures are commonly issued in a form that specifies in great detail exactly what programmes and/or populations are eligible, what actions must be taken to qualify for subsidization, and so forth. Both in their form and in their effect, many financial measures are difficult to distinguish from those usually called "regulatory". Our concern is not with this formal distinction but with exploring the dimensions of regulatory effects of financial instruments. A very simple way to look at the topic is to distinguish between effects on: (a) decision-making by subordinate or co-ordinate levels of administration and governance; (b) educational treatments of special populations; and (c) minority group education and status.

Effects on decision making

The extent of potential effects on decision-making for any financial incentive is, of course, a function of the degree of autonomy exercised by participants in the policy-implementation process, with respect to more direct regulatory measures. Thus, the greater the autonomy, the greater the potential role of financial instruments as opposed to other measures. It is not surprising, therefore, that financial measures play an extremely important role in situations like the Canadian and United States federal systems. The more important lessons to be drawn from the project data do not concern the acceptance of such obvious constraints by policy makers but, rather, the extent to which choices can be made. One set of choices occurs when the policy makers have the possibility of choice between financial and other measures, e.g. a change in the autonomy and freedom of choice of subordinate decision-makers. The second is the devices used, within a given set of constraints, to make financial measures flexible, effective instruments of policy.

The Canadian financial system provides an excellent example of the complexities of possible trade-offs. The use of a formula transfer scheme to provide revenue to provinces for bilingual education was an option exercised in the early 1970s; at that time, a relatively small component of the Federal financial incentives programme was placed in so-called special projects, arrived at on a jointly negotiated basis with the provinces. This system, which bears a marked resemblance to the Australian system of negotiated project budgets for Federal transfers to the states, implies a much higher degree of control over programme content than the formula transfers. The Federal pressures to change the balance in the funding system from formula payments to negotiated special projects, visible from the latter half of the 1970s, represents an attempt to introduce greater "accountability" for expenditures at the risk, if the Federal views are put into practice, that provinces will not make extensive use of the system. The "risk" would involve, of course, a much lower set of demands on the Federal treasury together with a shared control over programme content. At the same time, the extensive development of elementary and secondary educational systems in the provinces with the largest minority populations — Quebec for the English minority, New Brunswick and Ontario for the French — reduces the risk for minority language educational services in precisely those provinces where the greatest transfer payments occur. The provinces have opposed the system, and the minority Francophones have been left in a middle position — requesting greater accountability from the provinces for expenditures without endorsing the Federal position.

This example is quoted at some length to illustrate the main components of a typical situation:

(i) A triangular relationship between: a funding source; an agency or jurisdiction that receives the funds and administers educational programmes; and a minority that is the client of the programmes offered.

(ii) A funding source with partially contradictory policy objectives: a need to limit expenditures to the minimum necessary for achieving policy objectives; a set of legal or constitutional constraints on action; a set of power relationships in the political arena with the recipient agency and the minority; a set of educational and/or social policy goals defined in terms of services to the minority.

(iii) A recipient educational agency or jurisdiction with similarly contradictory objectives: a commitment to provision of service to different populations, including the linguistic/cultural minority(ies); trade-offs to make between services provided to the different populations; a need for revenues sufficient to permit the delivery of services; an investment of resources, both past and current, in the present system of educational services, any change in this system requiring that costs be incurred; a degree of autonomy which it is prepared to defend; a political situation involving dealings with the funding source and two constituencies (at least): a minority and a majority.

(iv) A minority faced with two alternative agencies, on whose decisions its educational provision depends and with whom its possibility of direct influence varies depending upon the situation.

Our earlier analysis of different forms of policy objectives found that the tendency in most situations studied was for the "higher" level agency to have a broader set of possible incentives for taking positive action to help minorities than subordinate agencies. This is usually accompanied by a greater access to taxation revenues at the higher level as well. The result is the paradoxical case where an agency at a higher level is often in a position to advocate for minority groups that are, strictly speaking, direct clients of the lower level agency. The niceties of political life dictate that, in many cases, the use of financial measures with various levels of incentives proves to be the least painful means of intervention to shift priorities of the lower-level agency.

In terms of degrees of optionality for the recipient agency, the studies reveal great variations. The highest degree exists where there is no specific constraint placed on the agency (except perhaps the demands of public opinion), the initiative for funding and programme creation is in the hands of the agency, and funding occurs in the light of very broadly defined programme delivery requirements. The least is where programme definition is centrally made and the resource flow is a by-product. In between one finds a number of hybrid forms. In Sweden, for example, regulations require local authorities to provide home language instruction for pupils whose parents request it, unless special authorization is provided centrally, the alternative being to purchase services from a neighbouring authority: this formal obligation is accompanied by a specific resource authorization based on funding for additional teaching time, an additional increment of time being provided for each eligible student; on the other hand, the form of the provision is left entirely in the hands of local authorities, since the numbers of students, their ages, and the possibilities for grouping vary between authorities. The French system is more centralized in appearance, since the decisions at all levels are taken within the administration; the provision of induction classes is left to lower levels of administration in the light of individual pupil needs and, since the numbers of eligible pupils cannot be predicted, the provision of additional teaching resources is not automatic; the creation of new teaching posts is taken on the basis of global shifts in posts, the exact allocation of posts not being done at central level: such a system increases discretion in providing service and permits the assessment of need to be tailored, so to speak, to fit the available resources.

The following are the key points on which policies differ with respect to the degree of choice left to the recipient agency or jurisdiction:

(i) *Initiation of service*, i.e. the decision whether a given programme of service will be initiated at all. In some cases, the decision to initiate a service is dependent upon receiving funds from the funding agency; this is a separate issue from that of whether the agency has the right *not* to set up the service under a given programme of finances. In Sweden, all local authorities are now required to provide home language tuition; in the United States, no school district is required to seek funds provided through the Bilingual Education Act on the basis of a provision in the act. (Court orders to set up a given level of service for a minority, of the kind issued against some local authorities, do not necessarily imply that the funding has to derive from the federal programme or, indeed, from any special source of revenue.)

(ii) *Choice of population and numbers served.* Some systems of financing have regulations defining strictly the categories of pupils to be served, who must be allowed to use the service, and so forth. Others are much less specific.

(iii) *Choice of mode of service.* The decisions involved here concern choice of instructional approaches, what types of staff may be used, the frequency and duration of instruction and so forth.

(iv) *Accountability and inspection.* Some systems of finance involve after-the-fact accountability either through budgetary controls or specialized reporting requirements.

One way of pointing out major differences of emphasis in funding programmes would be to rate the mechanisms used, taking into account the associated regulatory framework, on a scale of how much autonomous initiative and freedom from control is left to the recipient agency or jurisdiction. This is done in Table 8 for a variety of funding arrangements described in the study, using the author's own impressionistic judgement and the scale: H-High degree of independence, H-Medium degree of independence, L-Low or no independence. Where the terms of certain programmes are mainly left to negotiation between the funding agency and the recipient, i.e. where both have a say in the outcome, this is classed as "M", unless the constraints for negotiation are set in quite narrow fashion. The classifications are based in many cases on quite rudimentary data, so that the possibility exists for serious misinterpretation. Nevertheless, the system provides a relatively clear differentiation between funding arrangements. For clarity of presentation, the arrangements have been sequenced from highest to lowest degree of independence using a simple point weighting scheme (3 for H, 2 for M, and 1 for L).

Using this impressionistic scheme, the federal transfer systems of Australia, Canada and the United States are predictably in the upper sections where least constraints are placed on recipients. The United

Kingdom Rate Transfer Grants provide, of course, a maximum of flexibility but, as they are not specifically directed to education or to linguistic and cultural minorities, their placement in the same list is only for purposes of illustration, not direct comparison. The element of negotiation is the common characteristic of most of the other items in the upper part of the list, with the exception of the Canadian formula transfers and the Manitoba development grant, each driven by an automatic enrolment calculation. Predictably, the Western European continental countries are at the lower end of the list regarding autonomy of recipient agencies, but the differences with respect to Manitoba and the post-1978 system in Ontario are quite small, despite an entirely different structure for school administration. The French system ranks as being less constraining on lower level agencies largely because of the discretion in the system not to offer services to populations.

A final column indicates the extent to which funding automatically follows from initiating (or applying to initiate) a service or is dependent upon a central decision. The overwhelming majority of cases provide automatic funding, but the price of this is relatively low degree of discretion in the offering of services. Table 8 illustrates the extent to which some jurisdictions are moving towards mandatory special services for minorities with consequent automatic funding mechanisms. One anomaly in the list is the classification of the relationship of German *Länder* with respect to their local educational authorities (*Schulträger*); this might suggest incorrectly a uniform service structure for the country. But, of course, the major options regarding service offerings and modes are taken at the level of *Länder*, whose relationship with the Federal authorities is, in turn, quite autonomous.

Effects on educational treatments

The effects of financial instruments on the way that linguistic and cultural minorities are taught, cannot be separated easily from those of other policy instruments. As we have noted earlier, financial measures are often issued in forms that make them very hard to distinguish from "normal" regulations. In some systems where categorical funding is made available for costs such as teachers' salaries, the separation between funding instruments and other regulatory measures is, at most, merely nominal. The consideration of effects must, therefore, be done in parallel for financial measures and their accompanying frameworks of regulation and educational practices.

The reason both must be considered together can be seen easily from Table 8. In column iii, the amount of freedom left to funding recipients for

TABLE 8   *Classification of selected financing mechanisms in terms of freedom from central control for recipients of funds*

	i	ii	iii	iv	Funding Decision (1)
United Kingdom–Rate Support Grants	H	H	H	H	aut.(2)
Canada–Federal–Provincial Formula	H	H	H	H	aut.
United Kingdom–Section 11	H	H	M	M	cen.
Australia–Federal–State Grants	H	M	M	M	cen.
Manitoba–Development Grants	H	M	L	H	aut.
United States–Bilingual Education Act	H	M	M	L	cen.
Canada–Federal–Provincial Special Projects	H	M	M	L	cen.
Ontario (pre-1978)–formula	L	L	M	H	aut.
Manitoba–Maintenance Grant	L	L	M	M	aut.
France–Induction classes	M	M	L	L	aut.
Ontario (post 1978)–Added Cost Grants	L	L	M	L	aut.(3)
Sweden–Home language	L	L	M	L	aut.
Germany–Länder: Schulträger	L	L	L	L	aut.
Denmark–Home language	L	L	L	L	aut.

KEY: Extent of freedom from central control: H – High; M – Medium; L – Low.

    i Initiation of service
    ii Choice of population and numbers served
    iii Choice of mode of service
    iv Accountability and inspection after grant

(1) Funding decision on grant/subsidy:
    aut. Automatic funding if service is initiated
    cen. Central decision, often based on negotiation process.

(2) Classified as automatic because subsidy is entirely under control of local authority, once the grant is received.

(3) Decision on funds automatic, following approval of general plan for development of French language services in recipient school board.

N.B. All classifications based on limited data sources and subject to errors.

choosing the mode of educational service, is rated as "high" in only two instances; the "mediums" reflect, by and large, cases where negotiations occur or a choice can be made by the recipient within a usually restricted framework; the "lows" are almost totally controlled by existing policies and regulations in the systems concerned. The pattern of data does not suggest a fragmented decision making process but, rather, one where a choice is made to adopt a more or less strong regulatory stance with respect to funding recipients. Following this decision, a "package" of instruments is chosen to suit the strength of the stance and the policy objectives of the funding source. Keeping in mind that one is dealing not only with financial measures but also with a more complex regulatory framework, one can discern the *regulatory stances*.

Stance A.   United Kingdom Rate Support Grant and Canadian Federal-Provincial formula transfers.

Stance A provides maximum flexibility and has as one policy objective the reduction of interference by the funding source in decision making on types of service provided. The Rate Support Grants are not related specifically even to education. The Canadian formula transfers are based solely on the enrolment of members of official language minorities in school programmes where the language of instruction is their own; what the content of the programmes should be, is left completely unconstrained.

Stance B.   United Kingdom Section 11 grants, Australian Federal-State Grants, United States Bilingual Education Act, and Canadian Federal-Provincial Special Projects.

Stance B allows firm, final control over programme content but depends on decentralized initiative for programme ideas and initiatives. The financial systems are characterized by the combination of four elements: relatively broad central objectives, decentralized, non-mandatory initiation of programme or project proposals by potential funding recipients, a final central decision on whether funds will be granted, and a give-and-take process that involves formal negotiation or indirect bargaining between funding sources and recipients.

Stance C.   Manitoba Development Grants, Ontario pre-1978 formula, Manitoba Maintenance Grant, and Sweden's home language programmes.

Stance C is intended to ensure provision of services up to at least a minimum standard while leaving sufficient flexibility to avoid conflicts with other educational service priorities devised by funding recipients. It is characterized by three elements: mandatory provision of services in some form where a demand exists,[4] a range of optional forms of service defined by the funding source, the right of recipients to make a choice from among the options, and nearly automatic funding that virtually eliminates bargaining.

Stance D.   France's induction class programme, Ontario's post-1978 added cost grants, the relationships between the German *Länder* and the local school districts (*Schulträger*), and the Danish home language programme.

Stance D is intended to leave very little option with respect to the mode of service to be provided. The funding source may have a relatively clear list of options in prioritized sequence which the funding recipients are expected to adopt (Ontario) or exercises almost direct administrative control over subordinate decision making. Because it fits within a decentralized model of administration, the Ontario system is more open to "public" bargaining, but school board plans must be approved prior to funding. In the other cases, "internal" administrative negotiation may occur regarding specifics of implementation, recipients having some autonomy with choices at the level of school administration (assignments of teachers, rooms, pupils, timetables, etc.).

If one deals with these stances, rather than specific financial instruments alone, one can draw the following general conclusions with regard to relationships with educational effects:

(i) The stances allowing the greatest degree of initiative by the funding recipients (Stances A and B) are characterized by greater variety of programme form and programme content. However they are much less likely to result in uniform provision of services up to minimum standards for the majority of the potentially affected linguistic and cultural minorities.

(ii) Stance C making provision of services mandatory in some form, does ensure services up to a minimum standard; the crucial issue becomes the nature of the definition of the standard of service. In all cases the provision is centred around a definition based on use of a minority language for instructional purposes. The standard is thus quite variable, from a minimum of a certain number of hours of home language instruction combined with additional assistance in the majority language in Sweden, to a maximum in Ontario requiring 100% minority French language instruction (except for study of English as a subject).

(iii) Stance D provides very limited instructional options for recipients and results in reduced variety of programmes. It does not necessarily result in provision of services for all eligible members of minority groups. Whereas Ontario's recourse to strongly directive measures is aimed at attaining nearly universal provision, the other cases are situated at a different level of development, where coverage may depend, among other things, on central initiative in providing resources.

(iv) There is no clear relationship between the stance adopted and the levels of development of problem definition presented in an earlier section of this paper. The choices appear to be dictated initially by the constitutional or legal constraints placed upon funding sources, then by a combination of factors that are unique to each situation such as the administrative traditions of the jurisdictions and calculations of political opportuneness of the measures.

(v) The influence of financial measures (and other instrument choices) is much less important in determining the *type* of educational treatment than the level of development of policy objectives. The choice of financial measures and related regulations does have a strong influence on the *extent of implementation* of the policy, particularly in regard to accessibility for all members of the minority group.

The first three relationships [para. (i)–(iii)] do not appear necessarily generalizable to other situations. There is no reason why a strongly centralized approach equivalent to Stance D should not result in universal provision of specialized services for a given minority or group of minorities, provided that the policy objective is firmly set and pursued. Similarly even if Canada's Federal authorities have adopted an approach classed as Stance A, there has been a very strong development of educational opportunities for minority Francophones during the past decade; the approach took effect because of the strong national consensus on the topic and the agreement of the relevant provincial authorities to pursue parallel policies. The absence of such a consensus in the United Kingdom, combined with a regulatory approach of Stance A type, has led to a situation of relatively "spotty" coverage for immigrant needs in the different local educational authorities. Relationships (iv) and (v) are potentially generalizable and are deserving of further consideration in other contexts.

Effects on minority groups

The effects of financial instruments and their related regulatory framework on minority groups can be divided, at least in theory, into two classes: *indirect effects* are those that occur through the educational experiences received; *direct effects* derive from the immediate impact of the regulatory instruments on the persons and/or their position in society.

Direct effects. The pervasive nature of compulsory public education means that the conditions surrounding school attendance are both widely known in communities and deeply experienced by the persons affected.

Financial and other related regulatory measures can make significant differences to the status both of individual minority group members and of the group itself. The instruments can set up conditions for admission to education that may determine individual membership in the group. Australian public policy, including its educational policies, has adopted a definition for an Aborigine as "anyone of Aboriginal descent who identifies as an Aborigine and is accepted or regarded as such by the community in which he or she resides" (McKinnon & Bissett, p. 93). This definition is relatively broad, in that it includes persons of part-Aboriginal descent, and is neutral or non-pejorative. The United States Bilingual Education Act originally limited funding to programmes that served "children who come from environments where the dominant language is other than English". The 1974 revisions to the act changed it to refer to all children of "limited English speaking ability", a term that was revised in 1978 to refer to individuals with "limited English proficiency" (Leibowitz, 1980:17). Up until 1975 there was the further requirement that the children served must come from low income families (Palaich & Odden, p. 39). This example is typical of definitions that are based upon a deficit model of the members of a linguistic or cultural minority. Moreover, the right to remain in a "bilingual and bicultural" environment is, so to speak, conditional upon not overcoming the deficit. The nuances of wording are, in themselves, quite significant in their effects on individuals and their education. The 1974 revisions broadened the classes of individuals eligible for programmes but introduced a deficit concept for participation. The 1978 changes meant that an individual who had learned to *speak* English but who lacked other elements of linguistic proficiency (reading, composition and other classroom language skills) would no longer be prematurely removed from the programmes.

The examples are illustrative of the way that regulations related to resource provision can affect individuals by laying down precise conditions for the populations being served and for the personal characteristics of individuals admitted to programmes. In this respect, no definitional scheme is completely neutral. Admission to home language instruction for resident foreign workers in Europe is largely based on nationality, but the definition can have unanticipated effects, for example, if the home language is not the national language of the country (Turkish citizens of Kurdish language, Spanish citizens from Catalugna, etc.). The Canadian provinces have opted for definitions based on phrases such as "French-speaking students" but have not applied the definitions rigorously, as this would exclude children of French-speaking parentage who have been heavily Anglicized.

The effects of similar regulatory provisions on groups are also profound. Many educational programmes of a specialized nature are dependent upon renewed funding and, in many cases, funding is considered temporary or subject to non-renewal; disappearance of funding means the end of the programme, a situation that makes the status of the education of affected groups appear to be precarious. If the groups are also weak in a political sense, their continued educational special status can appear to place them in a dependency situation vis-à-vis educational authorities. The current United States legislation (Bilingual Education Act, as amended 1978), for example, recognizes this problem and places strict guidelines on the process of termination of grants to school districts (Leibowitz, 1980: 40–41). Non-renewal is, in principle, a possibility for any programme listed in Table 8 as not having automatic funding.

The negative connotations of the analysis given above should not obscure one fact: in many instances, even if the regulations surrounding funding have negative connotations in an absolute sense, the very existence of the programmes is often considered by the minorities concerned as a victory in their attempts to have their status and special needs recognized. Moreover, some of the regulations attempt in a positive sense to provide additional status or political leverage for minority groups. The latest revisions to the United States legislation, for example, require that applications for programme funding must be developed in consultation with an advisory council of which a majority are parents of children with limited English proficiency (Leibowitz, 1980: 39). Systems that tend toward long-term maintenance of minority groups usually have more thorough-going provisions that give the group members a formal role to play in the governance process, a point to which we shall return shortly.

Indirect effects. The main effect of regulatory measures on educational treatments, as we have seen, concerned the degree of implementation of policy and, in particular, the *accessibility of educational provisions* to the members of the potentially affected linguistic and cultural minorities. The importance of this effect is, of course, self-evident. The Canadian data indicates clearly the importance placed by the Francophone minorities on ensuring coverage of all their members through the quantitative expansion of amount of instruction in French both in terms of percentage of instruction given and of numbers of schools and classes. The discussion of minority aspirations in Section II has shown this to be a more general phenomenon, common to all the situations under study. On the other hand, one *caveat* must be introduced: the implications of incomplete coverage of the members of a minority group by a given type of educational provision depends entirely upon the *appropriateness of the educational experience*. To deal with one extreme, it is known that many indigenous peoples have experienced extreme effects of alienation both from their own social ethos and from the dominant values of the "modern" schools they attend. The extent to which this is traceable to the effects of schooling, by contrast with the general effect of social contact with a European-type society, cannot be determined, but there is no doubt that schooling does play a major role in this process. To turn to the situation of resident foreign workers in Western Europe, we can note that the models of educational experience pursued in different jurisdictions are sometimes based upon mutually contradictory assumptions. From the point of view of the minorities concerned, the value of universal accessibility to a given educational provision depends ultimately upon whether the assumptions underlying the provision correspond to their interests.

The reports indicate extreme variation between jurisdictions in terms of coverage and effects. In France, for example, only one out of five children of foreign workers has a generally "normal" school career; the German case study expresses severe doubts about the effectiveness of current measures; the results in the United Kingdom refer to unevenness of provision; the United States mapping study indicates that only a small portion of the target population is reached by bilingual and bicultural programmes. The most optimistic results are found in the Canadian case study. The fact that the latter refers to an established minority and the others to "new" minorities makes it unlikely that the role of regulatory measures is the main single causal factor. *The status of the minority appears, rather, to determine in large measure the regulatory approach adopted.* The overall impression derived from the studies is that the indigenous and new minorities are only poorly covered in most instances, and that the nature of the appropriate provision is not clear. Conversely, the established minorities are reached in much larger proportions. However, even in this case, there are wide differences as to priorities for content and the feeling of urgency for taking measures. As evidence one need only compare the strong emphasis on use of the minority tongue as the main instructional medium for Canadian Francophones, with the relatively weak role of the Welsh language.

From the preceding, two practical conclusions for action are in order:

(i) The regulatory stances adopted in many jurisdictions are failing to provide universally accessible minimum standards of service, particularly for indigenous peoples and new minorities. Because of the urgent character of the situation as reported, serious efforts should be made to improve breadth of coverage by using new regulatory stances.

(ii) Because of widespread differences in assumptions about what is the most appropriate provision for linguistic and cultural minorities, the search for appropriate regulatory stances should be accompanied by research and experimentation to determine the most suitable and effective educational programmes for affected minority groups.

Improved regulatory stances resulting in more universal coverage are not, alone, sufficient. If better coverage is achieved without better programmes, the result may be broad accessibility to inappropriate educational opportunities. Financial instruments have a crucial role to play, but only in relation to the broader regulatory framework adopted by each jurisdiction.

Notes to Chapter 4

1. Since completion of the case study for Canada, additional steps have been taken in Ontario to reduce the number of "mixed" secondary schools by creating French language "entities", i.e. independent French-speaking units with their own staff and quarters operating inside the same school building with an English language school. This is used where a separate school building is not practicable or desired.
2. Since the completion of the Canadian case studies, the separation at the level of local school authorities has been generalized in New Brunswick.
3. Churchill, p. 99; cf. Churchill, 1978, for full exposition of the theoretical construct for definition of level of educational services for minorities.
4. The Manitoba Development Grant does not require that the local education authorities choose any particular level of service; minimum standards are covered by law and regulations, and finance at any given level is provided by the Maintenance Grant. It is classified here because it fits within a larger framework making services mandatory.

5 Linguistic and cultural minorities in the governance system

policy instruments are the tools of policy making, which is the central problem of governance. Chapter 3 of this synthesis explored the major dimensions of societal and policy objectives from the perspective of the different groups concerned; Chapter 4 traced the inter-relationships between different types of policy instruments and options chosen by policy makers in the countries studied. The present section is devoted to the system of governance, that is the system used for defining objectives, choosing policy, and monitoring the implementation of policy. (This is what we termed earlier "external governance" to distinguish it from the more limited concept of "internal governance" or the regulatory instruments that are one of the options available for implementing policy.)

Our concern is with a relatively narrow set of problems surrounding the education of linguistic and cultural minorities, but these problems intersect with most of the major issues in the whole broad field of educational policy making. Many of the issues are treated elsewhere, particularly in the issues papers, the case studies of selected population groups, and the paper by Darnell on the analytical framework for considering the education of indigenous peoples. The purpose here is to focus on the empirical results of the mapping studies and case studies, to highlight common problems, and to raise, rather than resolve, major issues. These studies throw light on two broad topics: (i) the role of linguistic and cultural minorities in governance, the topic of this section, and (ii) rationales for policy making on the education of the minorities, which will be treated in Chapter 6.

Legal status of the minorities

Participation in educational policy making depends in the first instance upon the legal status of the persons concerned. The range in status in the different jurisdictions appears the greatest between the established and the "new" minorities; the indigenous peoples, on the other hand, usually have a special situation that is much less easy to classify on solely legal grounds. The major categories of legal status are based on rights to residence and participation in political life and, for the new and established minorities, can be arranged as follows, from greater to lesser legitimacy for participation in policy making.

Full national citizenship and established residence in a locality. This applies both to established minorities and to immigrants after an appropriate residence period. In most cases where decentralization of decision making prevails, residence for a certain period in a given locality is a legal, as well as practical, prerequisite to participation.

Full national citizenship without established residence in a locality. This applies to certain populations such as gypsies, barge dwellers, and various types of migratory workers (cf. mapping studies for the Netherlands, Sweden). In most countries, national citizens have a potential (not always realized) for participation in educational politics, even if lack of permanent residence may be an effective legal or practical bar to effective influence. In some federal systems, where voting rights in any type of election require the establishment of residence (with a few legally circumscribed exceptions), the lack of residence may effectively rule out any direct influence through the political process.

Qualified national citizenship. This status is most common among indigenous populations, whose rights have often been circumscribed by law. This particular problem will be discussed below. It also has been used in some cases to protect minorities by limiting rights of majority group citizens in some areas (Åland Islands, Indian reservations, etc.).

Non-citizenship with voting rights in local affairs. Recent Swedish legislation provided the first example of this, by extending voting rights in local elections to resident foreign workers. (A related form of voting rights has existed within the Commonwealth, depending upon the jurisdiction, for persons classed as British subjects but not holding national citizenship.) Because the import of the Swedish innovation is hard to assess at this early stage, it is ranked here as providing less formal status than different forms of citizenship.

Guaranteed right of establishment and residence without citizenship. This category has grown up as a result primarily of multilateral agreements within the EEC countries. A modified form of it exists within the Scandinavian countries and, on a bilateral basis, between former colonial powers and their former dependencies.

Conditional right of residence. The status applies mainly to foreign workers that reside in a country other than their own; in the EEC countries this applies to certain resident foreign workers originating outside the EEC. The right of residence granted to a worker ordinarily carries with it the right for members of the worker's immediate family to reside in the country as well. In cases where employment opportunities decline in the country as a whole or where the worker loses employment, residence permits may be revoked. As workers' families are now growing older in average age, the status of older children may be very insecure: there is at least one jurisdiction that has refused the right of residence to children over the age of 16 who are not employed, enrolled in an apprenticeship programme, or enrolled in school, i.e. deportation to their parents' country of origin.

Illegal aliens. Although not discussed in any of the reports in detail, persons who illegally live in a country and hold employment there constitute significant minorities in certain jurisdictions, particularly the United States. Such persons are usually subject to immediate deportation, often without right to hearing, if their presence and status become known. The desire to hide status may result in children being kept entirely out of the formal educational system or being withdrawn from it precipitously in order to avoid discovery of their parents' (and their own) status.

The status of indigenous peoples is a highly complex legal and political issue. It reflects a past in which, for the most part, the indigenous peoples were not considered capable of exercising their rights as full citizens or of defending their own interests. Practical and legal limitations have often been put on their rights and, in some cases, granting of citizenship is a relatively recent phenomenon. The limitation of rights has often been accompanied, on the other hand, by special privileges and protection not afforded "regular" citizens. Traditional systems of social order, including the right to limited forms of governmental autonomy (e.g. tribal or band government among North American Indians on reservations) and control of the resources or access to traditional homelands, have been preserved in some cases. Most of the jurisdictions studied in the project that have such peoples, show definite signs of having trouble arriving at a satisfactory definition of their legal status: The Ontario mapping study notes, for example, the existence of three separate groups: registered Indians — who enjoy the full set of privileges attaching to their status and whose education is the legal responsibility of the Federal government — and Metis and non-registered Indians, who are a provincial responsibility. Australian Aboriginal peoples are in a similar position of divided responsibility for their education. The overall picture of the status of indigenous peoples is one of qualified citizenship rights combined with, in some cases, special attention from authorities. The tutelage of the state over their welfare in the past has created a heritage of bureaucratic control that, quite independently of legal status, leaves most in a position of formal dependency upon decisions by others about their education and many other aspects of their lives.

Mechanisms for participation in decision making

The response of many jurisdictions to the weaker legal status of linguistic and cultural minorities and, where status is equal, to their numerical weakness, has been to develop mechanisms for associating them with decisions about the education of their children. The major forms of participation by minorities in the governance of education for their children include:

(i) *Direct influence through regular governance processes*: This involves ordinarily participation as electors and/or candidates for boards or nominated offices, acting in a role directly comparable to that of members of the majority. It is only accessible to minorities having the highest level of legal status. The extent of influence effectively exercised depends usually upon absolute numbers and on the local political/administrative traditions. The cases of greatest influence coincide either with areas where the minorities are a majority or near majority (e.g. in some Ontario school boards and some localities in Wales) or where the structure of decision making is itself divided along linguistic and/or cultural lines (e.g. in New Brunswick or Graubünden).

(ii) *Assigned special status or representation within the regular governance process*: In certain jurisdictions special representation mechanisms are set up, so that decisions concerning a minority must be dealt with in consultation with members of the minority, at their initiative or, at least, with their having some right to a voice. In its simplest form, this may involve reserving a limited number of seats or votes for use by minority group members within the regular organs of policy deliberation, e.g. one seat on a school board is reserved for parents of Indian children educated in the public school system in some localities of Ontario. The United States requirement that applications for funding under the Bilingual Education Act be vetted by an advisory council on which parents of affected children constitute a majority, fits into this same category; the same applies to the French Language Advisory Committees, whose advice must be heard by Ontario school boards that operate French language instructional units at the secondary level. A somewhat different approach is found in all three Canadian provinces studied, consisting in policies that reserve a certain proportion of administrative posts in the ministry or department of education for members of the minority, including very senior posts (Deputy Minister or Assistant Deputy Minister), and provide specialized sub-units or departments concerned with handling affairs of the minority group. The United States Bureau of Indian Affairs and the Commonwealth Department of Aboriginal Affairs are similar in function as specialized agencies, even if there is no requirement that staff be of the relevant minority group(s). In all these cases, a specialized mechanism is set up, either in representative organs of deliberation or in the administration, to ensure consideration of minority education issues.

(iii) *Control or influence over reserved areas outside the regular governance process*: Both in the United States and Canada, a portion of the schools for Native American Indians have been turned over to control by Indian tribes or bands, placing them in the orbit of the limited autonomy available on reservation lands. The extent of actual control is difficult to assess from the available data in the studies, but there is obviously a degree of external dependence because the funding of the schools originates from non-Indian sources and, in some cases, there is a need for external staffing.

(iv) *Control of or representation on specialized bodies outside the regular governance process*: New Zealand has set up with partial government funding the Maori Education Foundation and the Pacific Island Polynesian Education Foundation as well as a National Advisory Committee on Maori Education, all with strong representation of the minorities. The Australian federal government has helped set up Aboriginal Consultative Groups in all but one of the states; Manitoba has established three advisory councils, though with limited operations; in some jurisdictions (e.g. United Kingdom) voluntary organizations set up independently of government help may play, nevertheless, an important and quasi-official role in providing advice. The common characteristics of these bodies is their role outside the normal governance system with relatively limited competency and control over the main aspects of education affecting the minority. Their existence and function depend in large measure on the good will of associated authorities, which is apparently not lacking in most instances.

(v) *Tutelage by a third party*: The network of bilateral and/or multilateral arrangements growing up in Western Europe, under which national governments assume responsibility for funding and/or staffing portions of the education given to their nationals on foreign soil, effectively transfers responsibility for such matters in large measure to the relevant national government.

(vi)*Parental rights*: In the absence of any other mechanisms, most jurisdictions and educational institutions recognize the right of individual parents to be consulted about the education of their children, even if final decisions usually remain with the educational authorities. This is, obviously, an individual rather than a group right.

If one examines the list of forms of consultation and control available, in parallel with the localization of the different populations, it is clear that the first two forms (i–ii) are associated only with established minorities. Form (iii) appears to be quasi-experimental and does not touch the majority of indigenous peoples (though the Samit appear to have a larger proportion of their numbers in situations where their influence is strongly felt). Form (iv) is of importance with certain indigenous populations and, to a very limited extent, for some new minorities. However, the bulk of the populations categorized as *new minorities* and as indigenous peoples in the OECD countries appear to be in situations covered by cases (v) and (vi), i.e. *most minorities have little or no collective control or consultative role to play in decisions regarding the education of their children.*

Two attenuating factors should be pointed out: Firstly, the overall impression derived from the project as a whole is a growing tendency for jurisdictions to seek new forms of representation that permit minority groups to have some control over their education. The newness of the realization by authorities of the problems of education for resident foreign workers is, at least in part, a cause of the situation outlined. Secondly, even with strong good will on the part of authorities, creation of effective and useful consultative or decision making mechanisms for minorities is difficult and may require overcoming major obstacles:

(i) The numbers of a given minority in a given locality may be extremely small.

(ii) Several different minorities may be present in the same place, a situation common in larger urban centres. Finding effective means of representation may be hard, particularly if the minorities disagree among themselves about modes of representation.

(iii) Members of the minorities may lack experience in management of anything so complex as a modern educational system and, in fact, may have value systems that are at variance with the basic premises of the educational systems concerned.

(iv) Attitudes of surrounding communities and/or relevant professionals may create an environment where the use of minority opinions and consultative mechanisms may be ineffective or, at times, counter-productive.

Despite these and other obstacles, as we have noted, there appears to be a strong tendency to seek better and closer minority group involvement in governance. The impetus for this, in addition to broad changes in opinion that tend to accept greater diversity, has been the relative ineffectiveness of many programmes that lacked such involvement, particularly in dealing with indigenous peoples.

Levels of governance and locus of control

The earlier CERI study of primary school finance found that the jurisdictions reviewed had devoted particular concern to the problem of locus of control, that is the extent of local control or autonomy as opposed to central control of schooling. A major finding was a very strong relationship between the mode of intergovernmental finance and the level of local autonomy: "non-categorical modes of funding imply higher levels of local autonomy than do categorical modes" (Noah & Sherman, 1979: 59). Our own analysis has shown a tendency for governments to take a strong regulatory stance towards education for linguistic and cultural minorities, associated with a preference for categorical funding in all except one case. This raises the general issue of how minority education fits within the patterns of relationship between different levels of governance.

A review of the evidence shows that not one but a variety of factors have contributed to this adoption of stronger regulatory stances:

(i) In countries with relatively strong *traditions of central control* (i.e. "central" in terms of the country's individual constitutional structure), the stance is, one might say, a by-product of the normal system of operation. This applies, for example, to France and to the German *Länder* in their dealings with the school communities.

(ii) Central authorities have *privileged access to certain types of revenue*, therefore providing them with greater financial flexibility in responding to new problems. If a new problem is perceived (e.g. because of an influx of resident foreign workers), a locality operating within a fixed set of budgetary and staffing constraints may have difficulty in reallocating funds from ongoing programmes to create new ones. This is consistent with the mechanism noted in the early CERI study that erosion of local autonomy resulted in part from ever increasing demands for services whose costs "have tended to outrun localities' financial powers" (Noah & Sherman, 1979: 67).

(iii) The broad *geographic distribution of some populations* appears to dilute their presence in any given locality and to make it easier for central authorities to recognize their problems and to foster a co-ordinated approach. This is particularly notable in the case of the transfer of powers concerning education of Aboriginal populations from the states to the Australian Commonwealth through a 1967 referendum to modify the constitution. On the other hand, the central responsibility for some populations is not necessarily inconsistent with local administration and autonomy. The Australian and Canadian federal governments have both exercised their respective responsibilities for education of indigenous peoples through mechanisms that, for a large part, rely upon the states and provinces of their jurisdiction.

(iv) The *political influence of minorities*, where it exists, may be more strongly felt at more senior levels of governance, or its influence may be more consistently felt. Within systems that have ample autonomy at the local level, the pattern may be very uneven: some localities may prove very responsive to minority needs, whereas others are simply neutral and a few are hostile to them. Attention may focus on local "trouble spots" that involve resistance to minority rights, thus causing the local level to appear less responsive than it really is. The need to overcome individual cases of resistance may explain in large measure the strong regulatory stances of the Canadian provincial governments.

The development of minority education may run counter to certain attempts to decentralize educational control and promote local autonomy. In some cases, the minorities are small in number, so that development of specialized educational provision may require combining efforts in a number of localities, for example to get sufficient numbers together in one place to make it worthwhile to hire appropriately qualified teachers. Unless special financial and regulatory provision is made at a higher level, individual localities may not be in a position to carry out the task. A different kind of problem arises when the locality does not agree fully with policies of providing minority language education, or simply where local public opinion has not recognized the nature of the minority needs. The Canadian case study places considerable emphasis on the interplay between different levels of governance, in which minority spokespersons appeal to higher levels of governance to obtain intervention on their behalf. There is evidence of this also in other federal or decentralized systems, such as the United States and the United Kingdom. In both the latter cases, the central response has been to develop incentive-type financial programmes, as it has also been for the Canadian federal authorities. All of these incentive approaches appear oriented towards reconciling special assistance to minority groups with the dictates of a constitutional or administrative system that rules out direct regulatory measures in conflict with autonomy at the next level of governance. As noted earlier, the systems characterized by the greatest degree of local initiative are also those where there is the least uniformity in provision of services at a minimum level. Because the one notable exception (in Canada) coincides with a broad political consensus between provincial and federal governments on the need for minority language provision where numbers are sufficient, one must conclude that the underlying problem of local autonomy is that development of political agreement around the issue of provision for minority language education is difficult with large numbers of separate authorities obedient to local majorities.

The answer to the problem of potential conflicts between a local minority and a local majority has been found in some jurisdictions through the provision of direct autonomy to the affected minorities. The special forms of provision for minority involvement in decision making discussed in the preceding sub-section are all modes of reconciling such implicit contradictions between different types of autonomy. The limitations listed there to extension of such participation were mainly concerned with the characteristics of the minority groups. In terms of any major devolution of autonomy to a minority, it should also be remembered that there are immediate practical problems to cope with, particularly finance. Unless the minority controls significant wealth (for example control of natural resources by some indigenous peoples), special measures have to be taken to ensure resource equalization, analogous to those required for geographical equalization.

In summary, reconciliation of local control with the protection or development of minority educational rights has often proved difficult. In a few cases the provision of autonomous control of their own education for minorities has been adopted. The majority of jurisdictions have opted for strong regulatory stances combined with varying measures of minority participation in decision making.

Impact of minority participation in governance

Generalizations about the impact of minority participation in decision making about their own education are difficult to make on the basis of data available. Only the established minorities have acquired major degrees of group control, and it is difficult to generalize from their experience to the problems of other linguistic and cultural minorities. It is clear that established minorities attempt, wherever possible, to assert control over their educational systems and to expand their degree of autonomy. Certainly all groups share this same aspiration to managing their own destiny, even if this aspiration often goes unmanifested for a variety of reasons. At the same time, it can be observed that the most "successful" educational experiments are obviously those of the established minorities; however, the success can hardly be attributed to control of the educational system (to whatever degree it may exist), as these minorities also tend to possess numerous other attributes that may explain both their success and their acquisition of control — permanency, geographic containedness and various other characteristics discussed earlier.

A certain amount of light may be shed on the matter by taking the inverse of the question: the impact of non-participation in decision-making. Again causal effects are impossible to trace, as the very characteristics that lead to exclusion from participation are also those most likely to result in unsuccessful educational experience — impermanence, marginal socio-economic status and so forth. The pattern is, nevertheless, clear: The more "different" and the less "integrated" a group, the less is the likelihood of control and of educational success. Leaving aside the very particular case of the Samit, the indigenous peoples have all shown various degrees of difficulty resulting from extreme dependency on remote and alien bureaucratic systems. Despite a long tradition of well-intended efforts to promote education of indigenous peoples through decisions by specialized administrators and agencies, all jurisdictions appear to have begun adopting on at least an experimental basis, some forms of greater indigenous control. The new minorities, by contrast, have been hardly touched in most instances even by experimental schemes to permit their control. What is clear is that the present tendency to rely upon the home country governments of resident foreign workers for the organization of some parts of their education, will prove effective only so long as the intention of the workers is to return home. Should the objectives of these groups turn towards remaining as a minority in another country, a means will have to be found to keep in touch with their aspirations and, in particular, the aspirations of their children, socialized into totally new value systems and social conditions.

The impact of participation in educational governance appears to be indisputable in one respect: it helps create and strengthen the bonds uniting the members of the minorities affected. In some respects, the granting of a measure of control over education holds great symbolic value. Darnell notes that "decentralisation as an ultimate granting of authority is often seen by central agencies as a *tendency*, while indigenous minorities perceive it as an *event*" (p. 21). To the extent that one goal is to strengthen sense of community between members of a minority, organizing participation in education governance is one means of assisting it.

The evidence appears to support the following conclusions:

(i) Although no causal link can be demonstrated, there is a high degree of correlation between higher levels of minority participation in the governance process and higher levels of "success" by the minority in the educational system.

(ii) Mechanisms for participation by minorities in educational decision making appear to be generally recognized, though not necessarily implemented, as means to ensure a better match between educational provision and minority aspirations.

(iii) Minority participation in the governance process has as a major consequence the strengthening of community links among members of the minority.

6 Rationales for policy making on minority education

since special provision for linguistic and cultural minorities is well-nigh universal in the OECD countries, a general question arises as to what rationales are used in the governance process for formulating the related policies. Discussions of these issues are often confusing because: (i) individual policy documents may not be explicit about rationales or may leave some fundamental rationales or assumptions unstated; (ii) several dimensions of the same problem may be confounded or grouped together under one rationale. The first problem is common to most policy documents: the second has some unusual aspects that are closely related to the nature of linguistic and cultural minority problems. Thus, it is common to defend differential treatment of the minorities with arguments that do not distinguish always between three interrelated aspects of treatment; (i) differential pedagogy, that is the use of different languages, curricula or methods in teaching; (ii) differential allocation of resources; (iii) differential educational objectives and outcomes. A given policy may postulate, for example, that a minority requires a different pedagogical approach, that the approach costs more than usual forms of teaching, but set as the objective that the minority achieve the *same*, not different, educational objectives as the majority. Each of these dimensions will be treated separately below.

Background assumptions on language policies and costs

The case studies of linguistic minorities all include discussions on the background of language policies in the respective countries. The findings are remarkably similar, despite the other cultural differences that may distinguish Canada, France, Germany and the United Kingdom. All have inherited from the 18th and, particularly, 19th centuries, a general, widespread commitment to unilingual schooling organized on a territorial basis. The Canadian case study documents the attempts to suppress minority French language education in the three provinces, reflecting tendencies that were reversed in only the recent past; survival of minority language education in Ontario and New Brunswick appears to have been linked to the partial protection provided by the constitutional protection afforded to Roman Catholic Separate Schools and to the sheer impracticability of operating English schools in some localities where both staff and students were French-speaking. The 1870 Education Act in the United Kingdom essentially wiped out for decades the previously existing Welsh educational system in Wales. In both France and Germany, the use of a single language of schooling is intimately bound up with the development of the modern state and national feeling.

Against this background, current policies favouring differential treatment for linguistic and cultural minorities must be treated as a recent exception to a widely prevailing set of language policy assumptions common to all the case study countries as recently as the 1920s and 1930s. The place of Quebec within Canada meant, of course, that its system of government was obliged to come to terms with some forms of language co-existence, and Quebec itself set a strong example by the privileged place occupied in its educational system by minority English speakers. Canadian political structures had perhaps less to evolve than those of the other countries, but outside Quebec majority English opinion on language matters in education appears to have been similar. Moreover it is clear from the mapping studies that these background assumptions of public opinion were widely shared in the majority of OECD countries until quite recently.

One key effect of majority opinion on language policy is that, where significant numbers of minority group members are not part of the teaching profession (i.e. in all except a few jurisdictions), language policy attitudes become embedded in the activities of the educational system to such an extent that policy change requires a major shift in practices and attitudes for very large numbers of practising educators. Schoolroom practices are an effective, perhaps *the* most effective, form of educational language policy. Discussion of policy decisions and rationales within the governance structure should never neglect the fundamental role of educational staff with no formally assigned roles in policy making. Their views and assumptions form an invisible framework that structures such policy discussion, and the educational practices they follow, constitute *de facto* language policy.

Another important, but usually overlooked, set of background assumptions concerns the meaning of the word "cost" in speaking of educational costs. Drawing in particular on the issues papers by Rossmiller and Peston, we may distinguish between three main usages of the terms "costs" in policy discussions.

Costs for public opinion.   In the arena of public discussion, the most common use of the term "cost" is identical with the concept of "spending money derived from taxes". The nature of public debate and the procedures for appropriating funds for public services in most jurisdictions draws attention away from the costs of existing services and programmes, focusing it instead on scrutiny of additional expenditures resulting from increases in costs of existing programmes and, particularly, from addition of new programmes or services. Since educational services for linguistic and cultural minorities are relatively new and in expansion phases, attention is easily focused on these increased costs (Cf. Churchill *et al.*, 1978, for case studies of costs in local school board decision making).

Costs for the cost accountant.   One of the serious problems of cost management is to determine the amount of expenditure being made for any given service. Costing requires serious attention to relatively complex issues of financial assumptions, such as the amount of cost to be charged against a given service for such items as use of existing public buildings. The value of such costing approaches depends largely upon the suitability of the approach to the specific analytical or decision making task. So-called programme budgeting systems attempt to develop comparable costs for alternative programmes as a basis for arriving at fair-handed consideration of different service options. When applied to the creation or expansion of services for minorities, the use of these methods runs up against the extreme difficulty of arriving at an acceptable set of cost assumptions useful for comparing costs: educational systems are remarkably recalcitrant in conforming to the criteria of programme budgeting systems. Moreover, it is rare, if not unknown, even for very large educational jurisdictions to have an accurate costing model sufficiently complex to show the interactions of the different factors entering into cost evolution over more than a very short time period as a means of assisting decision making.

Costs for the economist.   Economic theory relies heavily on the concept of "opportunity cost" which may be defined very roughly as the value of what one gives up in order to adopt a certain line of action, e.g. the cost of creation of a new service is what one otherwise would have been able to do if the service had not been created. The concept is poles apart from the cost accountant's concern for such items as the historical cost of investment in buildings: if a building already exists and is unused, using it for a new service does not involve an added opportunity cost. The judicious use of opportunity cost concepts can help to clarify important issues in dealing with the provision of services to linguistic and cultural minorities. The issues paper by Peston considers, for example, what happens when one fails to invest in a service that will increase educational achievement for groups whose achievement would otherwise remain low: "What we are foregoing ... is the greater educational achievement of the less educable people. In other words, the cost does not disappear because resources are not committed for a particular purpose, they merely emerge in another form, and are borne by one lot of people rather than another" (Peston, p. 6). The relevance of such theoretical concepts to the reconsideration of the costs and benefits of the system of resident foreign workers in Western Europe cannot be disputed, and it is directly consistent with current re-evaluations of policy in various countries. This approach to costs also directly contradicts the concept we have labelled "costs for public opinion". "... in common practice the concept of cost is frequently taken to imply what new commitment is incurred when the *status quo* is changed. The decision to do something involves costs, the decision not to does not. In economics this is an erroneous proposition. ... a decision to help a special population certainly involves whatever it costs to do that. But a decision not to help that same population equally involves accepting as a cost its poorer educational performance" (Peston, p. 6).

In this discussion, we have juxtaposed two separate types of considerations: On the one hand, the framework of majority opinion in most countries regarding language policy is such that services for minorities are usually viewed as being a departure from the *status quo*. On the other hand, we have seen that the most common concept of cost used in debate on public services is one that focuses attention on expenditures generated by new services or, more generally, services that represent a departure from the *status quo*. Alternative cost concepts do exist, and the most theoretically satisfactory is one that contradicts popular political wisdom. In the discussion of rationales that follow, it should be remembered that a considerable amount of the problems in generalization result from the difficulty, when studying real, functioning educational systems, of disentangling the relative influence of sets of assumptions that are mutually contradictory but are an integral part of a single line of policy.

Rationales for differential objectives and outcomes

From the outset it should be said that most of the countries represented in the project pursue policies that are not aimed at achieving differential objectives and outcomes for members of the minority groups who are expected to remain within the respective countries. The rationales of these policies are not, therefore, rationales for difference but for achievement of common objectives, the same as are set for the majority. The topic of discussion is, therefore, the extent to which differential objectives and outcomes are allowed in policies that generally tend towards uniformity.

Chapter 3 presented a global overview of the main tendencies of public recognition of problems of linguistic and cultural minorities, including the assumptions made about problem causes, typical policy responses, and the implicit expectations for the future of the language of the minority in cases where it was not the language of the majority. At this point, our objective is to review this analysis, extend it in a few respects, and show its relationship to the other types of policy rationales — for differential pedagogy and differential resource allocation.

It will be recalled that the typology of problem definitions included models of objectives for six stages and one variant superimposed on the others: Stage 1: learning deficit, Stage 2: socially-linked learning deficit, Stage 3: learning deficit from cultural/social differences, Stage 4: learning deficit from mother tongue deprivation, Stage 5: private use language maintenance, and Stage 6: language equality. These models all apply to the situations where the linguistic or cultural minority are expected to be dealt with in the long term in the national educational system of their country of residence. The variant, labelled "migratory alienation", applies to persons such as the children of resident foreign workers, who may be expected to return to their countries of national origin.

Each model of problem definition carries within it assumptions about what should be the proper *educational objectives* to be sought by the minority group members and about the longer-term *social outcomes* towards which these objectives are expected to lead. The problem definitions in Stages 1 through 4 all posit that the minority should seek the same social outcomes as the majority, i.e. they should have the same right to benefit from participation in the social and economic life of the country as do the members of the majority. With regard to educational objectives, one may distinguish between instrumental and cultural objectives. *Instrumental objectives* are those that lead to commonly defined academic "success" (reduced dropouts, higher grades, higher number of years of successful retention in school) and, in turn, to greater chances in later economic life. *Cultural objectives* are those that relate to the individual's personal sense of place in the world, particularly as a member of a sub-group within society.

All of the first four stages are based upon the same instrumental objectives for the minority as for the majority. Educational success is ultimately measured by how well the student succeeds in the use of the majority language, in passing the same examinations as those passed by the members of the majority, and so on. They differ in the extent to which they acknowledge differential cultural objectives: Stage 3 acknowledges cultural differences and Stage 4 language differences, admitting the development of individual cultural and language capacities as part of the educational objectives of the system. It should be noted, however, that these cultural and linguistic differences are usually defended in policy documents for their instrumental value, i.e. they help to achieve the main instrumental objectives assigned to the educational system. The use of the minority language is viewed, therefore, as transitional, a stepping stone to acquisition of the majority language and culture. The variant model of "migratory alienation" is usually simply superimposed upon one of these four stages. In addition to the main objectives assigned by the relevant stage, children are given supplementary learning experiences in their own language and culture to permit them later to return to their home countries. This experience is usually viewed as being partitioned from the remainder of school activities, and at least from the point of view of their country of residence, the outcomes and objectives are those assigned in the country of national origin – in other words, they are being treated not as a minority but rather as members of their own national majority. This applies to the outcomes and objectives, even if educational practice rarely, if ever, permits them to achieve the same standard, unless the stay abroad is brief or they are in a very favourable family situation (Cf. Study by Wieczerkowski of German children abroad, cited by Ekstrand, 1980).

Problem definitions at Stage 5 and 6 levels involve significant shifts in objectives and outcome expectations. At Stage 5, private use language maintenance, the social outcomes remain very similar, in that minority group members are generally expected to succeed within majority society, reserving the use of their language and culture to "private" occasions. However this private use is added to the expected social outcomes as a recognized, socially valuable component. In turn, this implies a change in educational objectives, where, without eliminating the expectation that the minority members will acquire native-like abilities in the majority language and culture, the additional objective is added of developing the minority language at least to the level necessary for private use. Because of the dominance of the majority language in surrounding society (media, business, government), this implies extensive use of the minority language as the medium of school instruction. In turn this implies that examinations and similar measures of scholastic achievement are carried out in the minority tongue. Because the social outcomes of schooling are, by and large, expected to be the same for the minority as for the majority, modifications to learning objectives of school subjects are limited in areas of instrumental value and affect mainly topics directly related to the minority language or group culture (literature, history and social studies).

Stage 6 involves a major shift at the level of social outcomes assigned to education, in that individuals in the society are expected after schooling to have the opportunity to take part in one or more national cultures having approximately equal places in social life (give or take the effects of differences in absolute numbers of groups). The implications of this shift in outcome expectations are very great for the educational objectives set for students. Native-language acquisition becomes an important objective, more important than learning the second (majority) language. Within practical limits, the learning objectives set in the curriculum can be different, even for instrumental objectives (language objectives are, of course, different). Finally, it becomes difficult to talk separately of cultural objectives in the same sense as for the previous stages. Cultural objectives are no longer separate but are synonymous (in terms of group cultural objectives) with the instrumental objectives of education. In sum, there are two (or more) paths to educational success and two (or more) alternatives for social outcomes of education.

The relationships between problem definition models and objectives set for education are summarized in Table 9. The relationships have been described largely on the basis of their internal logic. Nevertheless, an examination of the policies pursued in different countries reveals that this internal logic is faithfully reflected, with minor variations, in practice. It should be stressed, however, that the viewpoint inherent in official policy is not always identical with the opinions of the affected minorities on the same policy. One close observer of United States policy development points out that, from the legislators' viewpoint, the reforms embodied in the Bilingual Education Act, are compensatory and intended to foster transition to English, but "the major proponents for them, especially those members of the ethnic groups involved in implementing the new directives, invariably refer to the programmes as bilingual/bicultural and see the objective as stable bilingualism with maintenance of home culture as well as the home language" (Paulston, 1978: 403). Under the impetus of the objectives held by the minority groups, educational practice may sometimes be pushed to serve objectives well beyond those officially set for programmes. A Swedish author notes, for example, that the proposals from an official committee that were used to develop current legislation, did not include suggestions for various forms of unilingual minority language instruction that have nevertheless been adopted as aims in several cities in Sweden (Ekstrand, 1980: 419). In a sense, these contradictions are normal for educational systems: official educational policies are embodied in educational practices which, depending upon the use made of them by the clients of the system, can be turned to many different purposes from those intended.

Viewed against the background of language policy in the majority of countries, the objectives explicitly acknowledged for policies reveal the strong persistence of earlier views based on assumptions of unilingual school settings serving an essentially unilingual society. Even though educational practice operating under Stages 3 and 4 may permit minorities sufficient leeway to pursue development of their group language and culture in a way corresponding to the objectives of a higher-level problem definition, policy statements and discussions tend to stress the objectives that are consistent with the unilingual/unicultural view, in which outcomes, instrumental objectives, and cultural objectives are presented as being the same as for the majority. From the viewpoint of the majority, the models may be grouped as follows:

Stages 1–4 –	integration of minority into majority society with minimal requirement of adjustment of the majority group to minority group goals.
Stage 5 –	acceptance of minority group maintenance in "private" domains, i.e. those where the majority group is not involved; otherwise, in joint activity areas (business, etc.) integration of minority into majority society.
Stage 6 –	acceptance of minority group as equal, implying adjustment of majority group to accommodate minority group in all shared domains.
Variants 1–4 (B) –	non-integration, non-contact with the minority whose members are assumed not to become long-term participants in the majority society or country.

The list reveals that, at least for the bulk of members of society, only Stages 5 and 6 require relinquishing of attachment to the value of a unilingual society. Stages 1–4 and the variants for migratory persons are, at least in principle, not in conflict with the majority society nor do they require it to flex — except in one area, namely the organization of schooling. From Stage 2 onwards, the models do require that schooling be changed, a fact which explains why the major point of surface contact and potential conflict between majority and linguistic/cultural minorities is the school system and why school politics occupy such a major portion of the energies of minority groups. Moreover the greatest degree of accommodation to these models is required of the professionals responsible for running education — administrators, specialists, and teachers. Each of the models implies a differential educational treatment, and it is the educational profession that is mainly responsible for organizing and implementing this treatment in practice.

The findings of this examination of objectives should be considered against the background of the earlier CERI study of primary school financing. It identified *equity* as a major policy concern of the countries studied, this objective being seen as the provision of access to supplementary resources for sub-groups with special needs. The current study confirms the existence of this general policy objective, but shows it to be much more complex than could be determined from data in the earlier study:

(i) All jurisdictions appear to recognize the applicability of the concept of equity to the development of policies for education of linguistic and cultural minorities. In general the policy goal of equity involves providing the minorities with improved opportunities of reaching the same educational outcomes and objectives as are attained by members of the majority. In a few jurisdictions, the goal is taken to mean helping the minority to achieve outcomes and objectives defined by the minorities in terms of their own aspirations and culture.

(ii) Even if all jurisdictions subscribe to a common general goal of promoting equity, their policies incorporate very different assumptions about the relationship of the minority to the majority. These assumptions are translated into policies that define expected educational outcomes and objectives in a variety of ways.

(iii) The implications of different outcome and objectives policies are a matter of great import for the members of minority groups, both individually and collectively. Completely successful attainment of the objectives can result, depending upon the jurisdiction, in consequences as different as the total disappearance of the minority as a group or its perpetuation as a major component of the national social fabric.

Rationales for differential educational treatment

At some point in the process of developing educational policies for linguistic and cultural minorities, decisions are made regarding the specifics of the educational provision to be offered — the programme content, student grouping, evaluation methods, language or languages of instruction, and so forth. These choices have been presented in the discussion of organizational arrangements in Chapter 5. Our concern now is to examine the underlying rationale — that is the problem definition and proposed remedies — implicitly or explicitly expressed in those arrangements. Obviously there is much interaction between the definition of problems and the definition of objectives, for the initial recognition of problems usually comes from examining the results of current educational practice and discovering its shortcomings. The detailed choices for educational provision remain, however, a sufficiently different, and partly technical, domain to merit separate treatment. Present practice has been defined in terms of the relationship of schooling with three elements of minority group existence: language, cultural characteristics, and community structure. Each has been linked theoretically both with individual and group development through the educational process.

Schooling and language

The main aspects of language-related problem definitions have been commented on already in Chapter 4, and the organizing dimension for categorizing models for different stages of problem definition was linguistic (cf. Table 5). Let us review these stages of problem definition in terms of the assumptions they imply about learning by bilinguals.

Bilingualism and learning handicaps. Stage 1 and 2 models view the mother tongue mainly as a handicap to school learning. This corresponds to the trends found in most early research on bilingualism, which was viewed as having negative effects on children, both cognitively and affectively (cf. research reviewed by Cummins, 1979). The viewpoint remains an important orientation both for many policy makers and for the views of some current scholars (cf. Ekstrand, 1980). Moreover, the general assumption that speakers of minority languages suffer a handicap as a result of their use of their mother tongue, carries over into other stages of problem conceptualization, up to and including Stage 5. This carry-over results both from historical evolution — most systems at one time based

TABLE 9 *Social outcomes and objectives of education in relation to stage of problem definition*

Problem Definition Model[1]	Expected Social Outcomes	Educational Objectives	
		Instrumental	Cultural
Stage 1: Learning Deficit	Same as majority: integration and success in majority society	Same as for majority: acquisition of majority language and success by same indicators	Same as for majority
Stage 2: Socially-linked learning deficit	Same as majority	Same as majority	Same as majority
Stage 3: Learning deficit from cultural/social differences	Same as majority	Same as majority	Same as majority but mutual cultural respect encouraged, differences acknowledged
Stage 4: Learning deficit from mother tongue deprivation	Same as majority	Same as majority	Same as majority but transitional use of minority language admitted as an aid to achieving instrumental objectives

Variant – Stages 1–4(B): Migratory alienation	In "new" country: Same as majority In "old" country: Same as majority	In "new" country: Same as majority In "old" country: Same as majority	Same as equivalent stage above, except that separate cultural experience added outside the main framework of schooling in "new" country
Stage 5: Private use language maintenance	Same as majority plus retention of culture in private social settings	Same as majority, except that success may be tested for at least part of educational experience; limited programme content variations admitted along with use of language for instruction	Same as majority but own language development pursued to level necessary for instrumental success and for private use, maintenance; special own culture topics included (e.g. literature, history)
Stage 6: Language equality	Different from majority: success in "own" segment of society, assumed equal to majority even if different	Different from majority: content may be different. Own language acquisition dominant over majority language	Different from majority: own culture assumed to be integral part of instrumental objectives

1. See Table 5, Chapter 3 for fuller description

policies mainly on a Stage 1 or 2 problem definition — and from the common tendency towards stereotyping and labelling of individuals in terms of perceived group traits — in this case the lower social status of many minority groups is also equated with lower cognitive abilities. To the extent that use of a minority language can be equated with a mental deficit, then the usual deficit-based rationales common to other areas of special education can be adopted with little modification.

Majority language mastery and school success.   The converse of considering the minority language a handicap is the equating of majority language knowledge with educational success. The most immediately perceptible element available to classroom teachers for determining children's scholastic ability is their estimate of the child's verbal ability in scholastic tasks. The undoubtedly strong correlation between verbal ability and general intelligence in most native speakers of a language, is well established. This gives rise to the assumption that the main problems of minority language children can be resolved by providing sufficient instruction in the second language. Problem definitions in Stage 1 through 4 all incorporate this rationale.

Mother tongue usage and mental development.   Stage 4 problem definitions incorporate the assumption that, particularly for younger children, use of the mother tongue is important for individual cognitive growth as well as the formation of self-concept. The use of the mother tongue in the school environment is viewed as a means of fostering this continued growth during the transition period necessary to acquire knowledge of the majority language. Many Stage 5 situations involve transition, at some point in the child's educational career, from a minority language to majority language schooling environment; for this reason, the rationale remains a live issue in systems which are not generally based upon a deficit concept of minority language usage.

Oral ability and language mastery.   A most serious issue in so-called transitional programmes is the decision with respect to the appropriate point at which to make a transition into instruction given almost wholly in the majority language. As noted earlier, modifications to the United States law were made specifically to eliminate the situation where children were transferred out of bilingual programmes as soon as they acquired good oral English skills and were no longer within the category of those having "limited English-*speaking* ability" (emphasis added). This corresponds to a refinement of criteria that, since they are not specifically mentioned in most of the data gathered for the project, may not have been introduced in other jurisdictions. There is research and theoretical evidence to support the contention, however, that development of skills sufficient for academic success in a second language beyond the early elementary years (where oral skills play a greater part) may require extended periods (cf. Cummins, 1980). It is uncertain whether some of the longer transitional programmes (e.g. in Bavaria, North Rhine-Westphalia, Sweden) emphasize this rationale.

The role of schooling in majority language acquisition. Stage 5 problem definitions have been applied mainly to established minorities and involve concern about the need to preserve a minority language group against assimilation. Among minority Francophones in Canada, for example, the development of progressively more unilingual educational forms in the minority language, appears based in large measure on the discovery that in their social circumstances, Francophones are so exposed to English language media and other contacts that the acquisition of necessary skills can be done through limited in-school instruction in the language as a subject. Conversely, the German case study points out the limitations of programmes in Germany where the students have little contact with the local inhabitants outside school and little other opportunity to acquire a knowledge of the language. These examples demonstrate that some instructional design explicitly is taking into account (and may well do more so in the future) the implications of out-of-school language acquisition.

Long-term viability of bilingualism. Programmes reflect assumptions about the extent to which bilingualism is a "normal" long-term option for members of society. Stage 5 and 6 problem definitions are based on the supposition that groups can maintain their language and culture for long periods, even when they differ from those of the majority. Stages 1 through 4 take the opposite approach, though Stage 4 systems often exist in situations where the minority already has a demonstrated longevity. From the viewpoint of the individual learner, the schooling situations fall into two distinct categories, characterized by Lambert (1975) as "additive bilingualism" and "subtractive bilingualism". Additive bilingualism occurs when a second language is acquired with the expectation that the mother tongue will continue to be used; subtractive bilingualism occurs when a second language is learned with the expectation that it will replace the mother tongue.

A brief inspection of the rationales underlying the different programmes reveals important, inherent contradictions. Depending upon the assumptions chosen as a rationale, entirely different educational treatments can be developed. These have been outlined in chapter 4 and the implications for the role of the home language summarized in Table 6. Programme design appears to be based upon three successive sets of choices: (i) assumptions about the role of language and minority groups in society, i.e. the general objectives for education discussed in an earlier sub-section; (ii) within the framework of these objectives, the choice of language-related rationales consistent with them; (iii) the design of arrangements appropriate to the local situation (numbers of students, relationship of minority programmes to other components of educational systems, availability of staff, etc.) with a view to achieving an efficient, effective programme for meeting the objectives set.

The majority of programmes for linguistically-defined minorities are created in the light of this schema. It is important to note that the main rationales invoked are language-related and linked to the appreciation of the instrumental value of the home language and majority language for achievement in the educational system. The relationship between these factors and broader problems such as the minority culture and community structures of minority groups, does not appear always to be clearly articulated or perceived, particularly in problem definition stages 1 through 4 (though 3 is a partial exception).

Schooling and culture

Educational programmes are adjusted to take into account the cultural characteristics of minority groups in a variety of ways, each with its implicit or explicit rationale:

(i) *Grouping pupils of same or similar culture.* Pupil grouping practices at the level of classroom teaching reflect a number of criteria, of which pupil culture is often one. In many situations, the definition of "culture" may be equated with language background, or language difficulties, but in others the criteria are specifically oriented towards grouping children with the intention of providing them with a compatible environment, particularly for initial transition into a new schooling situation.

(ii) *Eliminating negative elements in the curriculum.* Partly through the impetus of the human rights movement and partly through related multiculturalism concerns, many jurisdictions have undertaken the revision of textbooks and teaching materials with a view to eliminating negative stereotyping of different cultural and ethnic groups. Until recently, for example, the religions of many groups (other than the dominant groups in the relevant country) were presented in strongly pejorative terms (e.g. by use of terms such as "superstition" or "worship of ..." rather than "religion" or more neutral descriptive terms). More than any others, indigenous peoples have been adversely affected by negative views that so deeply permeate other cultures that total elimination of the stereotyping is impossible, e.g. because it is an integral part of the literary tradition of various countries.

(iii) *Sensitizing educational staff to minority cultural characteristics and needs.* Training seminars and other forms of training for teachers and educational staff dealing with minority group members, are a very common feature in most areas where such minorities live in significant numbers. Some components of training programmes are intended to provide information on the life, customs and expectations of minority group members; others are more oriented towards specific pedagogical problems such as how to deal with linguistic differences in the context of teaching. A few jurisdictions have made such training a regular component of pre-service education of all teachers (e.g. Sweden).

(iv) *Providing culturally-relevant information to groups other than the minorities.* A major component of multiculturalism programmes is the development of the knowledge base of persons not belonging to the minorities. Such programmes are reported both as in-school activities directed at children and as community outreach activities involving the populace at large. The programmes pursue multiple purposes: increased direct contacts between majority and minority, elimination of misinformation, and development of positive attitudes towards cultural differences.

(v) *Providing staff of the same culture.* Provision of staff from the same culture as pupils is done consistently when the curriculum involves teaching in the language of the minority. This practice is often extended to other groups where it is felt the children are insecure or unable to cope with the demands of adaptation to the classroom environment, particularly if their home environment is considered primitive or non-modern. In these cases, qualified teaching personnel may not be available, and there is extensive use of teaching aids and so-called paraprofessionals in several countries.

(vi) *Introduction of culture-related subjects into teaching programmes* or changing the content of such programmes. Certain relatively minor changes to the content of school subjects is often a by-product of multiculturalism policies and the elimination of negative stereotyping. Some programme changes go beyond this "cosmetic" approach and introduce totally new topics, either as special subjects or syllabuses or as sub-components of existing courses of study. The areas most affected are social studies, history and literature. The implications of the changes depend upon the clientele to which they are directed. A programme of "Indian/ Black/Hispanic/Asian/Mediterranean Studies" directed at members of an affected minority is a recognition of the right or need of the minority to learn about its own history and customs; a programme addressed to the majority in the same country, particularly if it is made obligatory, suggests that the minority culture has a long-term general relevance for all citizens. The encouragement of knowledge of the Maori language and culture in New Zealand as a part of the national heritage is an example of the latter approach. A variant of the former approach is found in a number of jurisdictions, where the teaching of "culturally-relevant" topics such as social studies, history and geography, may occur in the minority language.

(vii) *Recognition of the minority language.* The role of the minority language in schooling has been dealt with extensively already. At this point one may emphasize that, by most definitions, language is an integral part of culture, but that many multicultural programmes are intended to give a place of prominence in schooling to all elements of a minority culture, *except* its most prominent symbol, language. Most programmes of education for indigenous peoples across the countries studied, despite a number of experimental and limited attempts, do not accord any role to the indigenous language other than as an oral means of facilitating communication with very small children. Recognition of minority languages does occur for other groups in two main forms: recognition as a language of instruction for members of the minority and recognition as a topic of instruction for members of the majority. Making a minority language an elective subject for members of the majority, particularly if the minority language is not a "prestige" language, is a considerable symbolic step (as in the case cited for Maori); making it obligatory as a subject of study is usually reserved for cases of recognition of long-established minorities in a Stage 6 situation. (Note, however, the Canadian exception: the development of Francophone education has occurred in parallel with the elimination of French as an obligatory subject of study in secondary schools and universities.)

The above list, while non-exhaustive, comprises most of the forms of adaptation of educational treatments to the minority culture reported for the countries studied. The overt rationale in each case is relatively clear. Cutting across the different forms are important assumptions about the objectives of cultural adaptation of education and about the nature of minority cultures. The *objectives* are linked to the definition of the problem to be overcome.

Problem	*Objective*
1. Minority has difficulty in adapting to majority culture.	1. Facilitate transition of minority.
2. Minority suffers from discrimination and from negative attitudes of majority and majority culture.	2. Eliminate visible instances of negative stereotyping and discriminatory-type actions.
3. Minority suffers from non-equal status and lack of positive valuation of its culture.	3. Provide positive recognition of minority culture by majority society at large.

From the minority viewpoint, the first problem definition can be equated with a negative view of their culture and is based on the expectation that they are to adjust to the majority culture. The second definition is neutral or potentially neutral: the emphasis is on the elimination of overt injustice. In practice, the programmes for elimination of stereotyping are sometimes presented as means of helping the minority adjust to the majority culture and, obviously, the objectives are complementary. The third problem definition is positive, in that it places a positive value on the minority culture and seeks to find means of expressing this in formal ways. So-called multicultural programmes often include all three elements with different degrees of emphasis.

The *definition of culture* present in most programmes is rarely made explicit. It can be derived from an examination of the emphases of programmes. At the most negative, it implies that the home culture is a *"deprived" environment* or "primitive" and that the children are not accustomed to "modern" situations or to an environment requiring discipline and regularity. The emphasis of programmes resulting from this problem definition is on helping children to overcome the "handicap" of their culture and to learn the new culture and its demands. The definition is close to programmes that are labelled "compensatory" and is part of the rationale of approaches (i) to (v) above. The programmes involved, it should be noted, are not necessarily conceived as being directed at the population concerned on the basis of linguistic or cultural differences. United States Compensatory Education programmes funded under Title I, for example, are intended to compensate for environmental inadequacies that have led children to perform inadequately, and the legislation refers to the "special education needs of the children of low income families", a category that coincides in many cases with linguistic and cultural minorities; the Bureau of Indian Affairs is a major recipient of funds from this source (Odden & Palaich, pp. 20–31). In a certain sense, one may speak in many countries of a "culture of poverty" that, because it is often correlated with linguistic and ethnic cultural differences, contributes to the view of minority bilingualism or culture as a handicap.

A second operational definition of culture involves considering the home culture as a *topic of interest* or curiosity because it involves customs different from those of the majority. This definition verges on the folkloric and is not necessarily flattering for those concerned, but it lacks explicitly negative elements. It is often expressed in the warmest terms of human sympathy and understanding. The definition can be used as the basis of programmes intended to combat overt negative statements or actions directed at minorities and as a means of arousing the sympathy and interest of children and adults belonging to the majority. The emphasis is on human relations and attitudinal change within existing structures. Forms of programme listed above as (ii), (iii), and (iv) are closely related to this rationale.

Treating the home culture mainly as a topic of interest is, to a large extent, neutral in value. Other operational definitions are, from the viewpoint of the minority, much more positive. One involves recognizing the minority culture as an *enduring need for the minority* group members, i.e. as a part of their existence that cannot be removed or neglected without causing a form of prejudicial deprivation. The consequences of such thinking, in most modern social systems, are to recognize enduring need as a fundamental right. The most common recognition of this right is the provision of culture-related instruction either as part of the optional curriculum for minority group members or as an out-of-school activity. Obviously, recognition within the school programmes involves a higher level of official commitment in both symbolic and real terms. For various reasons, official recognition of the language of the minority as part of the commitment of the school has been rare until recently, even for established minorities.

The most positive, and most rare, operational definition involves a major shift in public attitudes for its accomplishment. The minority culture is considered an *enduring concern for the majority*. Modern educational systems were created to provide citizens with the broad minimum of knowledge considered necessary for them to understand their environment and to adapt to it. The implication of recognizing a minority culture as an enduring concern, not only for its own members, but for society at large, is that the compulsory educational system has a responsibility to impart a knowledge of its basic elements to members of the majority. This can involve serious changes to the content of programmes of study for the majority, mainly in culture-related subjects. The introduction of obligatory instruction in the minority language is, of course, the most constraining on the majority and is found only in a few cases of established minorities or multicultural states (Belgium, Finland, Switzerland, Yugoslavia and parts of Canada).

The relationship between the major forms of educational treatment that recognize the minority culture, the related objectives, and operational definitions of the minority culture are shown in summary in Table 10. Some of the major forms of educational response have been separated into two components, depending upon whether the responses affect only the minority or both the minority and the majority. One group of persons belonging to the majority is consistently affected by almost any measure affecting the minority: the teachers and other personnel of the educational system. Form (i) of educational response, pupil grouping, is common to many other of the responses; it is entered in the list only in its simple form, i.e. for the limited case of a transitional measure or when it is enduring and corresponds to streaming of difficult or anomalous students.

The juxtaposition of different elements in Table 10 highlights one very interesting reciprocal relationship between definitions of culture and the extent of recognition received. There is a strong tradition in education, according to which a topic of study acquires a special status if it becomes a matter of formal study and examination ("discipline" is the term sometimes used in English). The operational definitions of "handicap" and "topic of interest" for minority cultures, have a connotation that culture is a matter of personal behaviour, such as food, dress, and personal manners of socializing. The operational definitions that imply recognition as a subject of study are psychologically on a different plane and require conceptualizing the minority culture as something of general intellectual interest outside the confines of personal behaviour. Conferring status as a subject of study is a major symbolic act both for the minority and the majority.

A review of policies followed in different jurisdictions in the light of the above remarks calls for two generalizations:

(i) There is an increasing tendency across different jurisdictions to develop educational responses that emphasize at least a "neutral" valuation of the minority culture, that is encouragement of its being viewed as a topic of general interest and discouragement of negative acts or attitudes toward minorities. This tendency is usually complementary to measures to facilitate adaptation of minority group children to the majority culture and helps attenuate the negative connotations of culture shift.

(ii) Even though the tendency towards neutral or positive cultural valuations extends to all groups, the overall impression of treatments accorded to indigenous peoples is that they are still mainly based on a negative concept of their culture, have as a major component the objective of compensating for the home environment, and fail to include home language (including non-standard forms of the majority language) as a significant basis for intellectual development.

Schooling and group development

The relationship between a minority group and an educational system is often a crucial component in the network of social structures that shape the group's development and long-term survival. As we have noted, participation in the governance process can, for example, strengthen the links between members of a community. Because of the importance of schooling for this aspect of life of minorities, some educational policies include it as a specific rationale, among others, for special treatment. In other cases, even if the policy rationale is not formulated in these terms by the authorities, the political mobilization of the minority in order to obtain recognition and relevant educational treatment, means that the educational provision made is viewed by the members of the group in this light and has the same effects in spite of the absence of an official rationale. The major aspects of educational governance and school operations that are advanced in different jurisdictions as contributing to community development and to related schooling impact on minority children are as follows:

(i) *Participation in governance*, either in a direct decision-making capacity or in a consultative role. This ranges across a wide variety of forms, from nearly full control of governance for some established minorities, through various intermediate forms like band and tribal control of Indian schools, to modest degrees of consultation and involvement of parental groups in discussions leading up to decision making by authorities.

(ii) *Participation and visibility in school operations* as teaching aides, and volunteers or as full-fledged teaching or administrative staff. The more advanced forms of participation include such policies as that in Ontario of having minority-language supervisors for teachers belonging to the minority group and, in several jurisdictions, of having senior officials from the minority group. Conversely, even the use of minority group volunteers or salaried assistants in the classroom provides substantial "visibility" in the eyes of children.

(iii) *Pupil grouping* and separation from majority pupils, either at the level of the classroom, a portion of a school, or the school itself, together with pupil grouping in recreational activities such as sports.

Policies that involve these practices may be justified on quite different grounds from their impact on the social cohesion of the minority group. Even when this is a conscious aim, the justification varies. In jurisdictions where the aim of government policy in areas other than education is to foster the maintenance and/or development of linguistic or cultural minorities, group development may be advanced as a separate justification, in and of itself. This applies particularly to established minorities and to indigenous peoples. On the other hand, community development may simply be defended because of its impact on children's learning and the improvement of the outcomes of their school experiences.

Figure 3 presents in summary form the major relationships between the type of effects that such policies are suggested to have. Its components are as follows:

(i) *"External" participation mechanisms*: the different means offered to minority groups to participate in policy making through the political process.

(ii) *In-school participation and visibility*: the presence of minority group members in the capacity of "workers" in the school system, whether on a volunteer or salaried basis.

(iii) *Community effects*: the hypothesized increase in social cohesion between members of the social group resulting from both the activities involved in participation and from the symbolic value of knowing that such participation occurs. For groups that otherwise lack significant involvement in public affairs, participation in educational governance can provide a focus for mobilizing community energies and a forum for the development of leaders. When the socio-economic level is particularly low, the creation of

TABLE 10 *Operational definitions of minority culture and relationship to educational responses*

Operational Definition of Minority Culture	Valuation (Minority Viewpoint)	Provision Type	Objectives: emphasis			Groups affected		
			Adaptation of Minority to Majority Culture	Eliminate Negative Factors	Positive Recognition	Minority Group concerned	Education Staff (Majority Group)	Majority Population
Deprived Environment	Negative	i	x			x	x	
		v – a	x			x	x	
		Gen. Comp.	x			x	x	
Topic of Interest	Neutral	ii	x	x			x	
		iii – a	x	x			x	
		iv	x	x	x	x	x	x
Enduring Need for Minority	Positive	iii – b	x	x	x		x	
		v – b	x		x	x	(indirect)	
		vi – a	x		x	x	x	
		vii – a			x	x	x	
		vii – b			x	x	x	(optional)

Enduring Concern for Majority	Positive	vi – b	x	x	x	x	x
		vii – c	x	x	x	x	x

Provision types:

i	Pupil grouping (only), see text
ii	Eliminating negative curriculum components
iii – a	Staff sensitization
iii – b	Obligatory teacher training (usually pre-service)
iv	Information for majority about minority
v – a	Minority staff, initial transition (compensatory)
v – b	Minority staff, own programmes or language
vi – a	Minority subjects in curriculum for minority
vi – b	Minority subjects in curriculum for majority
vii – a	Minority language teaching for transition
vii – b	Minority language teaching for maintenance
vii – c	Minority language teaching for majority

Gen. Comp. General compensatory measures common to special education for those with learning disabilities.

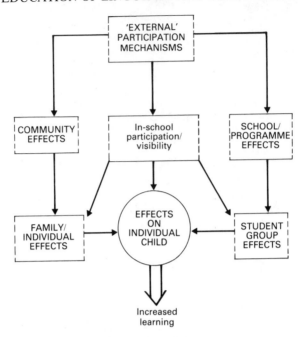

FIGURE 3   *Network of major effects of minority participation in school governance and operations on community and family*

even a limited number of salaried posts as teaching assistants takes on unusual significance.

(iv) *Family and individual effects*: the hypothesized impact on families and individuals in the minority group of participation, either because they feel more integrated into society generally or because they have better communication and contact with the educational system resulting in decreased psychological "distance" from schooling.

(v) *School and programme effects:* the changes in school activities and the programme of study resulting from minority group participation. It should be noted that the changes made do not have to be reflected in formal policy, such as a modification to the teaching syllabus. The presence of a teaching assistant in a minority class where children are learning to read in a second language may significantly modify the content and impact of teaching on the children.

(vi) *Student group effects*: the creation of cohesion between minority group students. The grouping of students into joint activities is one part of this. At the same time, the visibility of in-school participation by minority group members and the effects on schooling and programmes may further contribute to this cohesion. Where the students are of the same language group and the language of instruction is the same, this is hypothesized to increase the likelihood that the school linguistic atmosphere outside the classroom will be closer to the minority culture.

(vii) *Effects on the individual child*: the effects on the child and his/her learning resulting from the combination of all other factors. Among the hypothesized effects are, in addition to self-concept enhancement (whose relationship with school outcomes is weak), greater degrees of familial support, increases in family expectation for achievement, more appropriate teaching and programming, greater sense of participation in school activities, and, for cases where language development is a goal, greater propensity to use the minority language with peers.

Factors in selection of rationales

The rationales advanced for differential educational treatment are often inconsistent and sometimes directly contradictory between different jurisdictions. The main factor dictating the choice of rationales is universally the main societal objectives set out for the education of linguistic and cultural minorities. But, with this overriding constraint, one can see the action of differential problem definitions. The main axis of difference is the extent to which the problem definition involves social as well as pedagogical factors. Within the rationales for differential pedagogy based on language factors, one can easily identify those that centre on the role of language for individual cognition and those that view language within the social context of group communication. The same differences between individual and group emphases are also visible in the rationales based on culture and group development. In the latter case, this may seem a contradiction. But it is entirely possible to diagnose an individual problem deriving from larger social group causes and to treat it on an individual basis without attempting to undertake remedies to the community problems; for example, if children have trouble in adapting to the school because of their background, certain temporary transitional measures may be taken, such as limited pupil grouping with use of minority teaching assistants. For a variety of reasons this may be an entirely defensible and reasonable policy to adopt.

In many cases the choice of rationales corresponds to the extent of latitude left to those making the choice: educational authorities and educators may be confined in their choices to what can be accomplished within the confines of the school system. Some programmes obviously are only handled appropriately within broader decision making contexts. In other cases, failure to take into account broader social contexts in decision making can lead to reasoning that is, to say the least, subject to criticism. Thus, Canadian experiments with so-called early childhood immersion programmes are often cited illogically as a basis for suggesting programmes for minority group children in other countries (cf. Paulston, 1978 for instances and a critique). This is done without taking into account that the success of immersion in a second language from kindergarten onward was accomplished with children of the national majority (English speakers), coming from supportive home environments (they were volunteered by their parents), in a society where they were directly exposed outside school to large amounts of media broadcasts (radio and television) in their home language, and in the context of programme objectives amounting to additive bilingualism: they were to acquire a second language through temporary immersion, then revert to their mother tongue for upper levels of instruction. The results were viewed, however, solely in technical terms as a demonstration of a programme of switching from one language in the home to another in the school. Proposing these results as a basis for programmes intended to serve minority group children in an environment where all the social variables just itemized were exactly the reverse (a minority, non-voluntary recruitment without home support, paucity of outside-of-school media exposure in the home language, subtractive bilingualism with replacement of the mother tongue as objective) may be cited as an example of the possible dangers of generalizing rationales from one situation to another without considering the limits of the original rationale.

In summary, one may conclude:

(i) The main factor in choice of rationales for differential treatment is the overall set of objectives that are set for the educational process by the jurisdiction.

(ii) The rationales chosen vary significantly in their emphasis on the extent societal factors outside the school should be taken into account and on the balance between dealing with problems in school on an individual basis or as part of a group phenomenon requiring group-based remedies.

(iii) Because of the interaction between different social and individual factors of schooling, the generalization of rationales from one situation to another requires extreme care to avoid overlooking significant elements both in the original and new settings.

Rationales for differential resource allocation

The setting of differential objectives and adoption of differential educational treatments for minority groups is reflected in most jurisdictions by corresponding changes in resource allocation. The rationales for allocation present little of novelty in terms of general principles but are adapted at the stage of application to fit the specificity of the programme area concerned.

General considerations: equity, equalization, governance

To use the terminology employed in the CERI study of finance in primary education, the countries studied have attempted in their allocations of resources to keep simultaneously in view three policy goals: equalization, equity, and locus of control. In dealing with linguistic and cultural minorities, when there has been a conflict between objectives, means have been found to support equity considerations even if it meant contradicting the resource allocation methods used for geographic equalization or the governance methods employed to decentralize or move locus of control to lower levels of the government system.

If one asks for the underlying rationale for this trend as it is reflected in the data of the project, one finds that the general principles involved are essentially the same for linguistic and cultural minorities as for any other group. What is new in these events is the decision to apply these principles to the populations involved. The analytical framework proposed by Darnell for the consideration of education for indigenous peoples draws from the literature on education finance, seven concepts used for allocation of resources to serve the goal of equity: the foundation system, equal dollars per pupil, competition, fiscal neutrality (or negative concept), levelling, minimum attainment and full opportunity. These he relates in turn to the difference made by some authors between horizontal equity — equality of revenues for all children or the "equal treatment of equals" —

and vertical equity — greater allocation to those more deserving of attention or the "unequal treatment of unequals" (Darnell, pp. 17–18). The project results do not suggest the need to add additional concepts to the list nor do they reveal significantly different principles being applied than those widely discussed in educational finance literature.

Extension of the equity principle to linguistic and cultural minorities

Only a few decades ago, it would have been quite rare to find the principles of equity applied in educational finance policies for linguistic and cultural minorities in the fashion now revealed across most of the OECD countries. The extension of such principles to provide differential resource allocation for these minorities is part of a larger process of recognition of special populations. Authors using mainly American data identify three major periods in recognition of the mentally retarded: the pre-1940 "public menace cycle", where on genetic and other grounds, the mentally retarded were viewed as dangerous, immoral and criminal; 1940–60, the "education-welfare cycle", in which government took on increasing responsibility for special programmes for the retarded; and 1960 to present, the "civil rights cycle", in which court action has helped to establish the rights of the mentally retarded to obtain education (MacMillan & Meyers, 1979: 159).

Among the countries studied in the project, if one leaves aside the cases of very old established minorities, the application of equity principles was generally made first to persons suffering from conventional educational handicaps (retardation and various physical or perceptual handicaps) and only somewhat later to linguistic and cultural minorities. As noted earlier, the initial stages of problem definition for such groups appear to be rooted in a generalization of rationales originally developed for the handicapped to deal with the "handicap" of linguistic or cultural differences. The higher stages of problem definition are applications of different rationales of equal rights for members of different groups to obtain an education. The lower stages recognize the rights to individuals on a short-term basis, i.e. with the objective of eliminating the group by absorption of the members into the mainstream of society, while the higher stages recognize differences as a positive element and may encourage long-term development, even erosion, of the differences. The latter stages are linked, of course, to a political rationale regarding national political consensus and the role in it of established minorities. The different extensions of the equity principle for established minorities therefore go beyond the rationales for the handicapped.

TABLE 11 *Rationales for extending the equity principle to financial allocations, a comparison of linguistic/cultural minorities and the handicapped and retarded*

Rationale	Linguistic/Cultural Differences	Handicap/Retardation
1. Self-protection	Ignored or treated as potential threat to the body politic[1]	Ignored or treated as potentially dangerous
2. Welfare	Concern for welfare: recognition of linguistic and cultural origin as source of inequality	Concern for welfare of all members of society: recognition of responsibility for "weaker" members
3. Human rights	Recognition of rights for individuals of minority group	Recognition of human rights issues, extension of juridical protection to handicapped or retarded individuals
4. Group equality	Positive valuation of linguistic and cultural differences	No equivalent
5. National consensus and cohesion	Long-term maintenance of minority groups as part of national political consensus	No equivalent

1. Not applicable in jurisdictions having old, established minorities.

A simple comparative model is presented in Table 11. The human rights rationale may be applied both to minorities and to the handicapped or retarded by policy; the cases of judicial intervention for either group are mainly limited to the United States, but the recognition of rights to an education with special help and assistance is broad and nearly universal at least in principle. The formulation of the court judgement in the famous LAU case in the United States summarizes the problem: "... for students who do not understand English are effectively foreclosed from any meaningful education" (Cited by Paulston, 1978: 403). There appears to be no necessary movement of policies along the different steps in the rationale, particularly to the last step of treating established minorities as a permanent national feature and encouraging their development as part of a means for building national consensus and cohesion: in this respect, the majority of states show great reticence towards any such recognition. From the point of view of financial allocation, any of the rationales, except the first (self-protection) can be, and has been, used as a reason for extending the equity concept to linguistic and cultural minorities.

Rationales for specific allocations

The equity principle permits differential allocations to favour groups having special needs. It does not determine on what basis the allocations will be made. The rationale for payment should be distinguished from the basis of calculation. The *bases for calculation* found across the project are entirely consistent with those found in the educational finance literature for transfers between different levels of administration or governance: (i) *unit*: reimbursement for a designated unit of classroom instruction (teacher), administration and/or transportation; (ii) *weight*: reimbursement for each child on the basis of a multiple of regular per-pupil expenditures; (iii) *percentage*: payment of a percentage of the full cost per child; (iv) *personnel*: reimbursement of costs of designated staff; (v) *straight sum*: payment of a fixed amount per child served; (vi) *excess cost*: full or partial reimbursement of costs above those for regular instruction (Kakalik, 1979: 217).

The *rationales* for providing differential allocations using the above modes require that one postulate an extra need for resources. The following rationales are used by jurisdictions in dealing with the resource transfers for linguistic and cultural minorities:

(i) *No extra resource requirements*: In some jurisdictions the existence of linguistically separate educational sub-systems has been used as a basis for not providing specific allocations on the basis of the presence of either one group or the other in the schools. In New Brunswick this has been used in combination with a second rationale, (iii), below.

(ii) *Extra resources for additional teaching intensity or for special materials or services beyond the usual*: The main idea is that the special needs require greater intensity of teaching (lower pupil: teacher ratios, extra teachers, extra hours of instruction, extra-qualified and more expensive teachers), more expensive materials (difficulty of acquisition or development, smaller press runs for books, etc.), or special services such as transportation of sparsely-settled minority group members to a central point of instruction.

(iii) *Special costs of serving more than one population*: The emphasis here is not on the minority(ies) but on the problems associated with organizing parallel services for more than one linguistic or cultural group. This means that the intensity of instruction for each of the groups might be the same, e.g. no extra teachers or teaching time for the minority, but that the total effect might be to drive up costs; for example by splitting a small population into two different language streams, average class sizes might decrease for both groups. Similarly the costs may not be incurred at the instructional level but rather in administration (parallel lines of supervision for teachers, for example) or transportation.

(iv) *Costs for creating new services*: The initial start-up of teaching units or programmes may give rise to costs above those usually incurred by an educational unit during regular operations.

(v) *Compensation for out-of-school factors*: This is a slight variant of rationale (ii) above. The school for minorities may be called upon to perform services that majority groups obtain through means other than the educational system. For example, in the absence of media operating in the language of the minority, schools may sponsor recreational and cultural activities (theatre, films, etc.) for one group as an adjunct to regular schooling.

The majority of allocation systems are based on rationale (ii), mainly that special needs require additional teaching resources. The others, except for item (i), are variants that provide the flexibility required by some jurisdictions to accommodate various constraints of a political or practical nature affecting resource allocations.

General trends

With respect to rationales for financial allocation, we observe:

(i) The basic principles of equity used to justify differential resource allocations to linguistic and cultural minorities are essentially the same as for other groups.

(ii) The extension of the equity principle to such minorities has some elements similar to the historical process of dealing with special populations such as the handicapped or retarded, but the concepts of group equality and promotion of national concensus and cohesion appear to be applied uniquely (though not universally) to linguistic and cultural minorities.

(iii) Whereas the bases for calculating differential resource allocations for such minorities are the same as for other special groups, the rationales for the amounts to be allocated vary considerably. The majority of allocations assume, however, that the process of dealing with a minority's special needs requires the utilization of additional resources for teaching, administration, and other services. Other rationales include: special costs of serving more than one population, costs for creating new services, and costs of services that compensate for out-of-school environmental factors. In the special cases where the minorities control and run their own educational sub-system, there may be no assumption that linguistic or cultural differences engender additional resource utilization.

7 Summary and conclusions

Objectives and limitations of case study methods

The Series III studies of selected population groups consist of case studies of policies on linguistic minorities in four countries — Canada, Federal Republic of Germany, France, and England and Wales — and of a group of papers discussing major issues in the education of indigenous cultural minorities. For the purposes of this analysis, these have been completed by reference to information on cultural and linguistic minorities found in the Series I country surveys of current practice and to relevant theoretical positions in the Series II papers on principles and issues. Taken together, these papers constitute a rich, in fact unique, source of information on the development of educational policies in the OECD countries. Because much of the information is of a type generally not published in accessible forms, the data base provides the first comprehensive means of undertaking comparative study of educational policies as they are articulated in regulatory, organizational, and financial policy instruments.

At the same time, the limitations of this information should be emphasized: it is not intended to provide the basis for testing hypotheses in a quantitative manner. The data are seldom directly comparable. The enterprise as a whole must be viewed as a set of case studies. Case study methodologies are most useful for opening up new areas of research and defining the nature of underlying problems. They generate hypotheses rather than test them. As we stated in the introduction after outlining the major questions: "the answers given to these questions should be construed as working hypotheses rather than definitive responses".

The major questions raised in Chapter 2 of the study are all of a kind that do not call for hypothesis-testing conclusions but rather for an analytical effort to find underlying order in the data: commonalities across countries are described, and the analytical framework used for presenting common relationships is a major result of the study. The main purpose of this analysis and of this portion of the total project is to use a single policy area as a basis for extending our understanding of the policy making process. In the following, we shall review the results of the analysis in terms of the light they throw on policy making and implementation for educational and cultural minorities. This will be used as the basis for discussing the major long-term concerns for co-operation and research in this area of policy.

The policy making process

Chapter 2 of this paper reviewed the background to the study, including the previous CERI study of educational finance. The original data gathering framework for the case studies of linguistic minorities was presented, with a view to clarifying certain obscurities of terminology and, in the light of the data, a simple model of the relationship between factors and elements to be analysed, was presented. The model highlighted the importance of public support in the policy making process and the difference between "external" and "internal" governance, clarifying the fact that both internal and external governance systems are objects of the policy-making process, subject to modifications themselves. Major questions were raised for discussion concerning: the factors that affect the development and implementation of policy; the influence of different policy instrument choices; the modes of organizing educational provision for minorities, their implications, and the factors causing the choice of modes; the relationship of the minorities to the governance process; and the rationales or assumptions underlying policy choices.

Chapter 3 deals with the context of policy making. Minority group characteristics and the national historical and political situation were dealt with as background factors to policy making and to the formation of attitudes and aspirations. Certain minority group characteristics appear directly related to their educational treatment: length of establishment, geographic isolation, cultural isolation, geographic "containedness", political awareness and participation, and general demography. The factors do not all operate in the same direction, that is positively or negatively, in terms of promoting situations where better educational provision is made for them. The review showed, rather, the complexity of interactions with other national background factors. With respect to national factors, it was noted that a long-term evolution of opinion has occurred, resulting in a much greater tolerance for linguistic diversity and less emphasis on unilingual education; the evolution appears to have touched most countries studied. In addition to the rather well-known factor of differences in levels of governance between centralized and decentralized systems, the data suggested a major role played by the persistence of national administrative traditions in determining policy choices.

The analysis of opinions and aspirations dealt with three sets of actors: practising educators, the national majority, and the linguistic and cultural minority(ies) in each given situation. The importance of the views of educators was tempered by the recognition of the structural and political limitations on their role in policy making, which limit their autonomous role mainly to making choices that concern fulfilling the current objectives of the educational system and exclude them in most cases from actions that would introduce new objectives. In addition to the long-term tendency towards greater acceptance of pluralism, majority public opinion appears to be swayed by certain major factors that vary from jurisdiction to jurisdiction: the recognition that linguistic and cultural minorities have problems similar to those in traditional special education, internal social pressures in political life, and, a recent innovation, international intervention and commitments, such as those undertaken by EEC members. The vast range of aspirations among minority groups was partly clarified by presenting them in the light of a four level model of development of aspirations through different phases: recognition phase; start-up and extension phase; consolidation and adaptation phase; and multilingual coexistence phase. The transition through phases depends in large measure on the level of development of educational provision for the minorities. Phase 2 (start-up and extension) can include minorities with aspirations either to transition (or assimilation) to the majority culture or to group maintenance; there appeared to be no ready examples of groups in phase 3 who favour transition over group maintenance.

A key conclusion of the chapter was that a model could be formulated of the major types of problem definition underlying the policy responses of the jurisdictions in the study. The model involves six major stages: (1) learning deficit, (2) socially-linked learning deficit, (3) learning deficit from cultural/social differences, (4) learning deficit from mother tongue deprivation, (5) private use language maintenance (for the minority language) and (6) language equality. A variant on stages 1 through 4, called "migratory alienation", applies to those cases where jurisdictions feel that the children are likely to return to the home country of their parents (resident foreign workers' children). These problem definitions all appear to be easy to associate with general types of policy response in the countries studied. The model is interesting as a link in the policy-making process: the problem definitions presented are those that can easily be matched with the major "moods" of majority public opinion in the countries studied. The stages of problem definition provide a means of grouping policy responses across countries and comparing like with like for purposes of analysis.

Chapter 4 is a concentrated analysis of policy instrument choices, emphasizing two areas: organizational arrangements and the combined topic of financial instruments and regulatory stances. In dealing with organizational arrangements, the chapter discusses separately arrangements in jurisdictions where problem definitions are in stages 1–4 and those in stages 5 and 6, the latter two applying almost exclusively to established minorities. The profiles for established minorities appear consistent to a large extent; whereas the situation of new minorities and indigenous peoples shows little consensus in terms of organizational arrangements for instruction. A taxonomy of different degrees of official commitment to the home language of the minority (where this is different from the majority) shows clear differences between jurisdictions and gives results consistent with the model of stages of problem definition. Administrative arrangements were shown to have significant effects on various aspects of education such as recognition of minority needs and the way policy responses are implemented. In the case of established minorities, a clear tendency towards separation and specialization of administrative organizations, usually with minority group staff, was discernible. The administrative criteria for establishing separate teaching units for minorities were found to depend upon three different concepts of the right to an education in a minority language. The role of teachers and their supervision highlighted a major difference of status. Compared particularly with teachers of established minorities, those dealing with new minorities are in a particularly unfavourable situation. Support and ancillary services was a final area where very unfavourable situations appear to exist, except for established minorities.

Financial instruments and their role were grouped together with general regulatory instruments for two reasons: in practice the two are almost synonymous in some systems studies, and it appears that the process of policy making results in the adoption of a "package" of measures where finance and regulation are considered together. The objectives pursued in the choice of specific financial instruments were linked not to the technical basis of subsidy but rather to instrumental objectives, i.e. to the ensuring of compliance with policy objectives through the use of appropriate incentives, and it was noted that, in a broader sense, incentives apply as much in centralized systems as in decentralized ones. The discussion of the regulatory effects of financial instruments was based on a detailed grid examination of the degree of autonomy exercised by finance recipients in terms of four key areas: initiation of service to a minority, choice of population and numbers served, choice of the mode of educational service, and freedom from follow-up accountability and inspection. An examination of fourteen financial mechanisms selected from various jurisdictions confirmed that the majority of jurisdictions have opted for leaving relatively little discretion to finance recipients in terms of dealing with linguistic and cultural minorities but have accompanied this strong regulatory orientation with quasi-automatic funding. The major exceptions are found in financial transfers made in highly decentralized countries at the highest level (Canada, United Kingdom, Australia). The greater the amount of regulation, the more automatic the funding, and vice versa, was the most salient correlation between instrument choices.

The detailed analysis of regulatory functions of financial instruments resulted in the definition of four major groupings of jurisdictions according to what were termed "regulatory stances". These stances were then examined in the light of their effect on educational provisions. It was found that each stance could be related in general terms to the educational provision made available but not to the model of levels of problem definition. This was because a more or less strong regulatory stance can be used to accomplish the objectives of policy formulated in terms of all levels of problem definition. On the other hand, the regulatory stance did have a strong influence on the extent of implementation of policy and, in particular, the accessibility of the provision to all members of the relevant minority group(s). A separate area of influence of financial instruments and regulatory stances is the effect on minority groups. The indirect effects on the group are exercised through the educational provision they eventually receive (or do not receive); the fact that some stances result in higher or lower levels of accessibility to educational opportunities is, of course, a major effect. However financial instruments also often have a direct effect in that the regulations associated with them may determine who is eligible for educational provision and, because of the pervasive influence of education on public attitudes, may have significant effects in determining who is considered a member of a minority and what the status of the minority is in society at large. Definitions of eligibility based on a "deficit model" of minority group educational problems (the lower stages in the model of problem definitions) can have a distinctly stigmatizing impact. Independently of the precise interactions of different instruments and stances, the analysis concluded that the particular problems of indigenous peoples are among those most poorly dealt with in all jurisdictions.

Chapters 5 and 6 address the influences that, through the governance process, affect the instrument choices just discussed. The review of minority group participation in governance deals initially with the legal status of these minorities; it is evident that, except for established minorities, the bulk of individuals affected by policies are excluded on grounds of citizenship from official participation in many aspects of governance, despite one or two exceptional examples to the contrary. Where rights are linked to residence and/or permanency, even citizenship does not guarantee influence. Finally, one category lies outside the usual groupings: illegal aliens, whose numbers are significant in some jurisdictions and whose children, perhaps more than those of any other group, may be subject to disrupted educational experiences. Indigenous peoples occupy an ambiguous place, for many groups are just emerging from a situation that historically denied them full rights of citizenship but provided them with certain other protections and/or advantages linked to their special status. An examination of mechanisms for participation by minorities in decision making shows that the major opportunities for direct influence are reserved to established minorities whereas the vast majority of "new minorities" (resident foreign workers) as well as indigenous peoples are in situations where they have little or no role to play in decisions regarding the education of their children. The examination of governance effects did show that one of the most important effects of minority participation in governance was the strengthening of community links among members of the community.

The examination of rationales for policy making in *Chapter 6* is an attempt to reveal some of the implicit assumptions built into policy choices. The section is articulated around the degree to which different policies accept and/or foster differential treatment of minorities with respect to: (a) educational objectives and outcomes pursued; (b) educational treatments; and (c) allocation of resources. With respect to outcomes and objectives, a review of policies shows that, until the problem definition reaches stage 5, policies are based largely on the assumption that the goal of the minority is to attain the same objectives and outcomes as the majority; in stage 5 differences are admitted for areas related primarily to private use of language and maintenance of culture; only at Stage 6 does a significant shift occur towards promotion of differential objectives.

Rationales for differential educational treatment are examined in relation to three elements: language, cultural characteristics, and community structure. The language-related rationales used in different jurisdictions are often based on contradictory assumptions, traceable in the first instance to differing assumptions about the role of language and minority groups in society, i.e. the problem definitions rooted in majority attitudes. Within these assumptions, the choices of rationales appear to depend to a limited extent on different views regarding the nature of learning in bilinguals. Eight major ways of adjusting instruction to cultural difference are outlined; in turn, they are found to repose on four operational definitions of what is meant by a minority "culture", labelled as: (1) deprived environment, (2) topic of interest, (3) enduring need for minority, and (4) enduring concern for majority. These operational definitions can be scaled from negative to positive in terms of their valuation of the minority culture. This scaling corresponds to the problem definition stages and, when mapped against policy of the recent past, shows a tendency of jurisdictions to move towards positive cultural valuations. Finally, the implications of policy for community development of minorities is seen as an emerging area of policy concern. Community development rationales for policies are summarized in terms of a composite model showing the different hypothesized positive effects of policies, like enhanced minority participation in governance of education.

The rationales for differential resource allocation are not, in terms of basic principles, different from those found in dealing with other groups. The most interesting issue is how the general concern for equity has been extended to cover linguistic and cultural minorities. This is contrasted with the partially parallel process of applying the same principle to the handicapped and retarded. Certain strong historical parallels are present, but the application to linguistic and cultural minorities includes additional grounds not applicable to other groups.

The *final view* of the policy making process that emerges from this analysis is one where policy is rooted in societal assumptions about the role of linguistic and cultural minorities, based in turn upon historical factors, in which the strongest is the development of public education in the Nineteenth Century mainly in a context of linguistic uniformity. These assumptions result in definable types of problem definitions that are in large measure a function of the characteristics of the minority populations concerned and of the level of educational provision available for them at a given point in time. Minority aspirations depend, in turn, on the level of educational provision made at a given time, and the response to their needs is a function of their level of aspiration, a sort of circular relationship. The selection of policy instruments has been coloured by many factors but, in the end, it is clear that most jurisdictions have adopted strong regulatory stances to ensure the availability of provision at a level corresponding to general public assumptions about the roles of minorities and the consequent problem definitions. The details of the provision made correspond to this framework. The detailed examination of rationales used in policy making reveals great coherence and consistency between policy actions and underlying assumptions.

A unified model of policy and practice

The search for common patterns in the data gathered for this project has resulted in the formulation of a number of descriptive taxonomies. An examination of these partial results, summarized in the figures and Tables presented throughout this report, reveals what is, on the surface, a surprising degree of consistency in the results — surprising because of the variety of countries and populations involved and because of the absence of any initial hypotheses suggesting the orderliness apparent in the data. Based on the data available it appears possible to formulate a relatively broad set of correspondences between different sub-components of the taxonomies in such a way as to create a unified model covering a finite domain of policy making: the development of policy for linguistic and cultural minorities in highly industrialized western societies. All major elements of the data for all countries studied enter into the model, except for one set: the data dealing with regulatory stances, presented in pp. 84–104, a point to which we shall return shortly in formulating general conclusions.

The "key" to the regularity in the data can be found in two sets of attitudes, corresponding to the majority and minority opinions in different jurisdictions. These appear to be the driving "forces" behind the policy making process. In Table 12, the levels of minority aspiration from Table 4 are mapped against the levels of majority problem definition from Table 5. It will be seen that for the first three levels of problem definition, minority aspirations are in what was termed the "recognition" phase, i.e. the bulk of minority group political pressure is towards obtaining recognition for its needs in terms that are minimally acceptable to the minority group's collective "self-concept". The stage of a minority push for quantitative development (level 2) occurs when the majority group's problem definition has reached at least stage 4, which implies a minimum of positive valuation of the minority tongue's role in cognitive development. The model of minority aspirations then bifurcates: those groups that reach level 2 and choose integration stay at that same level; only those that opt for group maintenance as a collective goal then move onwards to level 3, the consolidation and adaptation phase. This corresponds to stage 5 of the problem definition. The multilingual co-existence phase of minority aspirations only exists in jurisdictions where the majority problem definition has reached stage 6, language equality.

The factor that provides the causal link between these two sets of attitudes appears to be the current level of available educational service. In the majority of the jurisdictions considered, the minority appears to define its objectives in terms of a staged improvement in the *status quo*, i.e. the

TABLE 12 *Majority problem definitions and minority aspirations*

Problem Definition	Minority Aspirations
1. Learning deficit 2. Socially-linked learning deficit 3. Learning deficit from social/cultural differences	1. Recognition phase
4. Learning deficit from mother tongue deprivation	2. (a/b) Start-up and extension phase
5. Private use language maintenance	3. Consolidation and adaptation phase
6. Language equality	4. Multilingual co-existence phase

bulk of effort is concentrated on seeking a modest improvement over what exists. A few exceptions exist, primarily among old, established minorities whose aspirations go beyond not only existing educational services but extend to the whole role they play within their country or jurisdiction; this would apply historically, for example, to minority Francophones in Canada or to Catlugnans prior to the end of the Franco régime. (Individuals may always have aspirations going well beyond those of the group; our generalization deals with group behaviour under "normal", not "revolutionary" conditions.)

Table 13 presents a mapping of the problem definition stages against the operational definitions of minority culture presented in Table 10. The

TABLE 13 *Problem definition and operational definitions of minority culture*

Problem Definition[1]	Operational Definition of Culture	Cultural Valuation	Language Assumptions
1. LD	Deprived environment	Negative	Subtractive
2. SLLD	Deprived environment	Negative	Subtractive
3. LD-SCD	Topic of interest	Neutral	Subtractive
4. LD-MTD	Temporary need for minority	Neutral-Positive	Subtractive or equivocal
5. PULM	Enduring need for minority	Positive	Additive
6. LE	Endurng concern for majority	Positive	Additive

1. See Table 12.

mapping works exactly for all items except stage 4 of the problem definition, learning deficit from mother tongue deprivation. This corresponds to a definition of culture not found in the original table of responses to culture, i.e. one where the culture — and particularly language — is viewed as a temporary need for the minority. Two additional columns are also included: the cultural valuation from Table 10 and a new column where the language outlook of Table 5 is expressed in terms of the type of bilingualism using the terms of Lambert: additive and subtractive. There is a clear, regular consistency in the categories, with level 4 appearing as the transition level where majority problem definitions and cultural assumptions begin to acquire a positive aspect, as viewed by the minority.

Up until this point, the mapping has concerned underlying attitudinal assumptions. Table 14 relates these to the policy process, i.e. the formulation of objectives in terms of general social outcomes and educational objectives (Table 9) and to the rationales used in extending the equity principle to linguistic and cultural minorities (from Table 11). In turn, Table 15 relates the problem definition to what may be called "dominant" policy responses. The variety of specific responses across different countries is sufficient, when viewed at the detail level, that there are probably exceptions to every categorization; however, the table presents in summary form the most common policy response. The role of the home language (from Table 6) shows a straightforward correspondence. The adaptations made to accommodate the system to the pupils' culture follow a similar pattern; this is outlined already in Table 10 and, since the correspondence with problem definitions is clear from Table 13, need not be repeated here. Certain other aspects of policy response also show a certain pattern of correspondence: at stage 5 and 6 of problem definition, policy responses are found in terms of pupil grouping patterns (a prioritized hierarchy favouring increasing degrees of separation from the majority during instruction), provision of specialized support services (increasing degrees of complexity approaching levels for the majority), and concern for linguistic separateness of the administrative structures of education.

The different components of Tables 12–15 are related via the "key" of the problem definition categories. Because of the regularity of the correspondences found, it would be possible to transfer all elements of these tables to a single, uniform matrix, together with many additional subcolumns from the earlier Tables. While an interesting exercise, such a Table would obscure, by its very complexity, the underlying simplicity of the policy process: the data clearly indicates the over-riding role played by majority opinion within a democratic framework, hardly a surprising finding when expressed in such simple terms.

TABLE 14 Problem definition related to social and educational objectives and equity principles

Problem Definition[1]	Social Outcomes	Educational Objectives		Equity Extension Basis
		Instrumental objectives	Cultural objectives	
0. Historical	—	—	—	Self-protection
1. LD	Same as majority	Same as majority	Same as majority	Welfare
2. SLLD	Same as majority	Same as majority	Same as majority	Welfare
3. LD-SCD	Same as majority	Same as majority	Same as majority	Human rights (and welfare)
4. LD-MTD	Same as majority	Same as majority	Same but limited use of language	Human rights (and welfare)
5. PULM	Same as majority but private culture difference	Same with limited variation	Same with language support	Human rights/group equality
6. LE	Different	Different	Different	Group equality/National consensus and cohesion

1. See Table 12.

TABLE 15   *Problem definition related to dominant policy responses*

Problem Definition[1]	Role of Home Language in Instruction	Linguistic Separation Administrative	Special Support Services	Pupil Grouping	Cultural Adaptations
1. LD 2. SLLD	i. No encouragement	Little or no concern	Limited or non-existent	Trend unclear	See Table 10 for detail
3. LD-SCD	i. or ii. Encouragement outside school hours				
4. LD-MTD	iii. Short-term transition iv. In-school subject v. Long-term transition				
5. PULM	vi. Official language of instruction	Limited concern	Moderate provision		
	vi. Separate system	Administrative separation		Prioritized forms favouring separation	
6. LE	vi. Separate system	Administrative and/or governance separation	Developed provision		

1. See Table 12.

General conclusions

The regularity and obvious logic of the unified model presented above permits us now to summarize *the main conclusions of this report*.

(i) The OECD countries have universally responded to the needs of linguistic and cultural minorities by defining them as special populations requiring special educational measures. This is a relatively recent phenomenon and corresponds both to an international current of opinion and to specific circumstances in each country.

(ii) The policy responses of the OECD countries to the educational needs of linguistic and cultural minorities correspond to a rational process of policy formation in which the main driving force is the dominant view of majority public opinion in each jurisdiction. At a given time, public opinion holds a dominant general definition of the nature of the educational problems faced by minorities; this definition is then reflected both in policy objectives and specific educational provisions made.

(iii) The problem definitions, policy objectives and educational provisions made across the different jurisdictions studied, fall into relatively clear patterns that may be grouped into successive stages or levels. Whereas there is nothing to suggest that a given country or jurisdiction must move from one level to the next in terms of its problem definition and related policy response, the data suggest that once the decision is reached to make a policy change favouring minority aspirations, this corresponds to a move "up" the hierarchy in a regular pattern.

(iv) The choice of specific regulatory stances and instruments does not appear to be related to the nature of the problem definition but rather to unrelated factors such as national governance traditions.

(v) The choice of regulatory stances and instruments does have important effects, primarily in terms of the degree of accessibility to a given type of provision for the minority. The "looser" the regulatory stances, the lower is the likelihood that the provision will be universally accessible to the affected minority(ies).

(vi) Whatever the policy objective pursued, the jurisdictions studied all appear to have opted for relatively "strong" regulatory stances in dealing with linguistic and cultural minorities (relatively strong in terms of each jurisdiction's own usual practices of educational governance).

(vii) The nature of the educational provision made is much more strongly determined by the nature of the problem definition used in any given jurisdiction than by the choice of specific policy instruments.

(viii) All indications are that the effectiveness of the educational provision made for minorities falls far short of the goals set by policy makers in all jurisdictions, except for the treatment of some established minorities. In other words, linguistic and cultural minorities still have major, unsolved educational problems that will make this issue a continuing concern of policy making for many years to come.

Policy concerns and future co-operation

The most important question to be asked about a policy making process is whether it deals adequately with the problem it faces. The picture that emerges from this analysis, is of a policy making system that operates systematically and rationally within the framework set for it by society: there is evident consistency between the general trends of majority public opinion, the educational objectives set for education of minorities, and the corresponding educational provision made for the minorities. At the same time, this orderly picture stands in strong contrast with the depth of the unmet educational needs of the minorities. Except for the older established minorities, the educational results obtained by present measures are universally dismal, far below the corresponding standards in the surrounding majority societies. The root question is: why has the educational policy making system not eradicated this problem or, at least, brought it within more manageable bounds? In the answer to this question lies the promise for developments in the future.

One response should be rejected immediately, namely that educational authorities have not recognized the problems of minorities. Quite the contrary, the evidence is that the educational system is perhaps the *first* major societal institution to recognize the existence of problems related to linguistic and cultural minorities. The compulsory nature of public education means that the schools have to deal with all the children of the relevant age groups in a minority; there is no escaping this confrontation with the daily needs and demands of the children. Teachers and educational administrators are in the front lines of the battle to cope with minority needs.

A second response is only partially correct, namely that the problem is a new one. In some jurisdictions, some of the minorities are new — e.g. the resident foreign workers in many European countries. However (again excluding older established minorities), old or new minorities all share the same problems, at least as measured in terms of educational results; only certain differences of degree are evident. The recognition of these problems and the pursuit of the goal of equity for such minorities through differential treatment and differential resource allocation, are relatively recent phenomena, even for minorities that have been in place for long periods. The willingness to address the problems appears to be more closely linked to changes in the goals set for education by society, than to the length of existence of the minorities. The newness of some minorities is a partial answer to the question, but it is by nature temporary: if educational measures do not change their situation within a few short years, the problem will soon be both old and unsolved. Already some jurisdictions are facing the problem of dealing with third generation "new" minorities.

We have thus rejected, to a large extent, two possible explanations of the persistence of minority educational problems: blindness of educational authorities to their needs and the newness of the problems. Authorities are aware of the problems, and the problems are not new. Functionally the explanation is to be found in the nature of the governance process for education, as we have seen it through the analysis in this study. The governance systems of all jurisdictions involved have been designed to be responsive to the needs of the majority of people in their respective societies, and the analysis has shown this response to be consistent even for dealing with minorities. In some cases, the educational response to minorities is in advance of public opinion to a certain extent, but the politicized nature of relations between ethno-linguistic groups and their surrounding societies sets strict limits on how far educational systems can go in responding to minority needs. The root issue is how far societies outside the educational system are willing to modify their views of the roles of linguistic and cultural minorities within their countries. Educational systems cannot respond to minority needs unless societies are prepared to respond to those needs.

The data in this project show important promise for the future: the most promising indication is, of course, the major cross-national trend of opinion that, we have noted, has led to much greater emphasis on cultural pluralism in the entire OECD area. In terms of rationales, for example, we have noted a recourse to definitions of minority cultures, that are generally more positive than in the past. The analysis points to the need to concentrate efforts on a few key issues that may help to prepare the way for better responses in the future and that are fruitful areas for co-operative international effort.

(i) The monitoring of results in minority education is not systematic or consistent, either within countries or between them. Systematic efforts should be made to develop a clearer picture of the nature and depth of the educational problems, both nationally and internationally.

(ii) The minorities are, by and large, disenfranchized and unable to control the education of their children. The systematic development of means for consulting minorities and permitting them to participate in the process of decision making about their education appears to be a priority. On the other hand, knowledge about the different forms of participation available, their effects, and the potential for generalizing them to different situations, is extremely limited.

(iii) Most of the common problem definitions applied to the education of new minorities and indigenous peoples are rooted in deficit or handicap models of causes. Research on causes that does not include the broader societal context of education, is not likely to aid in changing this situation. A systematic effort is required to develop a better information base regarding the nature of minority problems in education with a view to encouraging public understanding of their relationship with general objectives of social policy.

(iv) The serious educational problems of minorities are often shared by the educational personnel who deal with them. The training opportunities and support for teachers fall short, in many jurisdictions, of what could be considered even a minimal requirement. Efforts should be made to get greater information on the needs of teachers in minority situations, to promote better training opportunities for them, and (where the teachers are not from the minorities) to associate with the role of teaching, members of the minorities affected.

(v) The problems of indigenous peoples stand out as the most difficult and intractable faced by education today. Priority should be given to the study of their needs, placing emphasis on their own role in defining the needs. The tendency to deal with indigenous cultures in education as if their cultural base did not often depend upon a different language or upon a different register of the majority language, raises serious issues requiring study. The relationship between language needs, indigenous cultures, and current schooling is very poorly known.

The list of issues presented here is centred around problems of research and information exchange. They are not, as such, immediately political issues, but they do hold great potential for throwing better light on political issues and for pointing the way towards more adequate educational provision. The nearly universal recognition of minority educational problems in the OECD countries and the willingness to look for solutions, is a major finding of this study. But the conversion of its results into practical solutions requires further work and application.

Bibliography

References in the text are of two types, with date of publication, or without:

(A) Without year of publication: reference is to papers issued in the OECD/CERI project which appear in the first list below under the appropriate series.

(B) With year of publication: reference is to a document or publication produced outside the project, which appears in the second list below.

A. PROJECT DOCUMENTS
SERIES I. COUNTRY SURVEYS OF CURRENT PRACTICE.
COUNTRY STUDIES.

K. McKinnon and K. Bisset	*Australia.*
R. Benson and W. Burtnyk	*Canada (Ontario).*
K. Hjorth	*Denmark.*
K. Burgin	*England and Wales.*
A. Labregere	*France.*
P. Siewert	*Germany.*
T. O'Cuellenain	*Ireland.*
M. Molenaar	*Netherlands*
M. Burns	*New Zealand.*
K. Eide	*Norway.*
A. Castelo Branco	*Portugal.*
O. Wennas	*Sweden.*
A. Chappot	*Switzerland.*
S. Dede	*Turkey.*
A. Odden and R. Palaich	*U.S.A.*

SERIES II. PRINCIPLES AND ISSUES

E. Lövgren	*Identification.*
P. Dague	*Identification.*
J. Blackburn	*Rationales.*
E. Hansen	*Rationales.*
K. Eide	*Autonomy.*
N. McKeon	*Autonomy.*
L. Ingham	*Autonomy.*
K. McDonagh	*Service Delivery.*
J. Hannaway	*Service Delivery.*
R. Rossmiller	*Costing.*
M. Peston	*Costing.*

SERIES III. STUDIES OF SOME PRIORITY GROUPS

a. Linguistic Minorities. Country Studies.

S. Churchill	*Canada (Manitoba, New Brunswick, Ontario).*
L. Limage	*France.*
H. Boos-Nünning	*Germany.*
H. Rosen	*U.K.*

b. Indigenous Cultural Minorities.

F. Darnell	*Analytic Framework.*

Commentaries:

C. Bourke	*Australian Aboriginals.*
W. Demmert	*Native Americans.*
A. Smith	*Maoris and Pacific Islanders.*

OVERVIEWS

W. Donovan, A. Fordham and G. Hancock. *Overview Report on Cross-National Project on the Financing, Organisation and Governance of Education for Special Populations.*

Stacy Churchill. *The Education of Linguistic and Cultural Minorities in OECD Countries.* (This document).

B. OTHER DOCUMENTS REFERENCED

BRATT-PAULSTON, CHRISTINA, 1978, Rationales for Bilingual Educational Reforms: A Comparative Assessment. *Comparative Education Review*, 22, 3, 402–19.

CERI, 1983, Questions concerning Educational Policies Towards Migrants in Certain European countries, Education Committee and Governing Board of the Centre for Educational Research and Innovation, CERI/ CD(82)22, June 1983.

CHURCHILL, STACY et al. 1978, *Costs: French Language Instructional Units. An In-Depth Study of Selected School Boards.* Toronto: Ministry of Education, Ontario.

COUNCIL OF EUROPE, Recommendation 928 (1981), Thirty-Third Ordinary Session and Assemblée Parlementaire, Rapport sur les problèmes d'éducation et de culture posés par les langues minoritaires et les dialectes en Europe, Council of Europe, June 1981.

CUMMINS, JAMES, 1979, Linguistic Interdependence and the Educational Development of Bilingual Children. *Review of Educational Research*, 49, 2, 222–51.

—— 1980, The Entry and Exit Fallacy in Bilingual Education. *NABE Journal*, 4, 3, 25–60.

EKSTRAND, LARS HENRIC, 1980, Home Language Teaching for Immigrant Pupils in Sweden. *International Migration Review*, 14, 409–27.

KAKALIK, JAMES S. 1979, Issues in the Cost and Finance of Special Education. In DAVID C. BERLINER (ed.), *Review of Research in Education, 7.* American Educational Research Association, 195–222.

LAMBERT, WALLACE E. 1975, Culture and Language as Factors in Learning and Education. In AARON WOLFGANG (ed.), *Education of Immigrant Students, Issues and Answers.* Toronto: Ontario Institute for Studies in Education.

LEIBOWITZ, ARNOLD H. 1980, *The Bilingual Education Act: A Legislative Analysis.* Rosslyn (Va.): National Clearinghouse for Bilingual Education.

LITTLE, ALAN & WILLEY, RICHARD 1981, *Multi-ethnic Education: The Way Forward. Schools Council Pamphlet 18.* London: Schools Council.

MACLURE, STUART 1972, *Styles of Curriculum Development.* Paris: CERI/ OECD.

MACMILLAN, DONALD L. & MEYERS, C. EDWARD 1979, Educational Labelling of Handicapped Learners. In DAVID C. BERLINER (ed.), *Review of Research in Education, 7.* American Educational Research Association 151–94.

OECD, 1983, Migrants' Children and Employment: The European Experience. Paris: OECD.

PORCHER, LOUIS 1981, *The education of the children of migrant workers in Europe: interculturalism and teacher training.* Strasbourg: Council of Europe.

NOAH, HAROLD J. & SHERMAN, JOEL D. 1979, *Educational Financing and Policy Goals for Primary Schools. General Report.* Paris: CERI/ OECD.

RIST, RAY C. 1980, The European Economic Community (EEC) and Manpower Migrations: Policies and Prospects. *Journal of International Affairs.*

SEMMEL, MELVYN I., GOTTLIEB, JAY & ROBINSON, NANCY M. 1979, Mainstreaming: Perspectives on Educating Handicapped Children in the Public School. In DAVID C. BERLINER (ed.), *Review of Research in Education,* 7. American Educational Research Association, 223–79.

SKOLÖVERSTYRELSEN (National Swedish Board of Education) 1979, Memorandum 1 (13): Organisation and planning for home language instruction and auxiliary Swedish lessons in compulsory school. Stockholm: SÖ, May 1979.

SWAIN, MERRILL 1981, Time and Timing in Bilingual Education. *Language Learning,* 31, 1, 1–15.

Index